MW00782160

THE RUNES REVEALED

AN (UN) FAMILIAR JOURNEY

Written by Ingrid Kincaid

Illustrated by Lara Vesta

INKWATER PRESS

Scan QR code for
more information on
this title

Copyright © 2016 by Ingrid Kincaid

Illustrated by Lara Vesta

Cover and interior design by Emily Coats

All rights reserved. No part of this book may be reproduced or transmitted in any form or by any means whatsoever, including photocopying, recording or by any information storage and retrieval system, without written permission from the publisher and/or author. The views and opinions expressed in this book are those of the author(s) and do not necessarily reflect those of the publisher, and the publisher hereby disclaims any responsibility for them. Neither is the publisher responsible for the content or accuracy of the information provided in this document. Contact Inkwater Press at inkwater.com. 503.968.6777

Library of Congress Control Number: 2016907860

Publisher: Inkwater Press | www.inkwaterpress.com

Paperback ISBN-13 978-1-62901-349-7 | ISBN-10 1-62901-349-8

Printed in the U.S.A.

3   5   7   9   11   12   10   8   6   4

ᚠ ᚦ ᛗ ᛏ ᛚ ᛁ ᛘ ᛢ ᚹ

Nothing is as it seems.

Tucked away on a hilly, cobbled lane, slightly below street level, and wedged between crooked, stone houses, there once was and perhaps still is, a tiny, easily-overlooked shop mysteriously named the (un) familiar.

19 Candlemaker Row, just south of
Grassmarket and Cowgate, in Old Town
Edinburgh, Scotland

The locals claim that it regularly appears and disappears. Perhaps you will stumble upon it yourself some day. I once did. It was the autumn of the year 2003.

In truth, I suspect it appeared for me because I was being called there by a wand displayed in the shop window, a wand of twisted wood topped with a citrine crystal. However, the shop was never open. The sign on the door declared that the shop's hours were based on whim and fancy, which in fact was quite true, for during my month-long stay in that ancient city, I returned again and again, called by the wand in the window, only to be disappointed by the locked shop.

Finally, one last visit before my departure proved successful. I stepped down several worn stone steps and into the tiny shop. My presence, when added to that of the shopkeeper, made the space feel crowded.

I asked to see the wand in the window. He gently removed it, laid it across the palms of his hands, held it out to me, and said, "It's you."

Or at least that is what I thought he said. The look of confusion on my face told him I did not understand. He repeated, almost in a whisper, "It's yew. It's made from the wood of a yew tree."

It was yew and it was me.
It was familiar and yet unfamiliar.
I carried it home in my hand luggage.
It has been my companion for many years.
It was my companion, long ago, in times past.
It is and has been a guide for me on this
(un) familiar journey with the runes.

THIS BOOK IS DEDICATED TO
THE (UN) FAMILIAR THAT EXISTS IN US ALL

CONTENTS

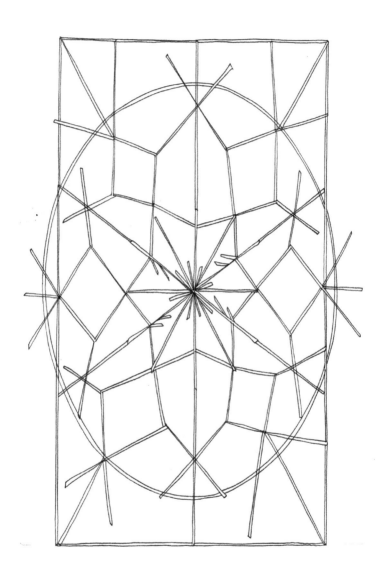

MY JOURNEY

Nothing I say is true.
Everything I say is true.
The truth lives in the questions.

My experiences and journeys with the runes are not and never have been conventional or ordinary. I have never studied them. I just know them. Or perhaps more accurately, I remember them. That being said, this is not a book based on historical writings or academic studies or exhaustive research.

It is a book about relationship, my personal relationship with the runes.

It is a book of questions.

When I close my eyes I see them as multifaceted, living beings, unique and individual, each one with its own personality. They hang in the cosmos like crystals, vibrating with sounds that encompass entire volumes of wisdom. They are not flat. They are not an alphabet. Their angular shapes are woven into the pattern of the Web of the Wyrd, the Web created by the Nornir who dwell in the roots of Yggdrasil.

Each rune has its own unique design and at the same time, the runes form and inform each other, creating all manner and combination of shapes, their lines crossing and intersecting, undulating and connecting, not on a flat plane but rather in a multidimensional matrix.

It has been a real challenge for me to write this book. I

have waited a long time. At first I justified the waiting by telling myself that there were already enough books written about the runes. But that really was not the truth. It was more about the fact that the longer I lived with the runes, the less I knew about them. They were constantly changing, hiding and revealing, and just when I thought I knew something, I would realize I did not. So how could I write a book about that?

What I have also seen with closed eyes is that the number of runes is unable to be counted or even grasped. I have written about 33 of them, just a small sampling at best, nine more than the 24 runes of the Elder Futhark that most people recognize and are familiar with. I sense that the additional nine belong somehow to the Jotnar, those giant, primordial beings who are often discredited and maligned. The 24 are a handful, the handful that Odin claimed he had the right to grab and remove from the Well because of his sacrifice. In fact there are some people who say these 24 runes belong to Odin.

There was and is no need to remove runes from the Well or the Web and claim them as our own. In fact, that is not even possible. We have been misled by the lie that we should be eternally grateful to Odin and fooled into believing that we should call him All Father.

We people of the runes are not monotheists.
We do not need someone to hang, starve and stab himself

so we can gain access to the runes, any more than we need someone to die for us so we can be saved.

The runes have existed throughout eternity, long before Odin came on the scene, and their wisdom is accessible to all of us. Each one of us has the ability to connect with the runes, to know them. It takes patience and a willingness to see in the dark and listen in the silence. Once we begin to recognize their shapes, we can begin to develop a relationship with them and the wisdom they embody and once we begin to recognize their sounds, we can fine-tune our own lives and allow the runes to play the music of their wisdom through us.

You can learn about the runes by reading a book, or by studying someone else's specific definition of what they believe a certain rune means or does not mean. But to know the runes you must form relationships with these sentient beings, and that is easier said than done. It is not just about you.

When a rune stave appears, whether in a reading, a casting or a drawing, whether in a crack in the sidewalk or the crook of a tree branch, or the flight of birds, you must first be still and go inside and ask yourself, what might this rune be trying to tell me?

And then you must listen.

And then you must be quiet.
It takes time to hear the answers.

Do not get caught up in worrying about whether a rune is upright, reversed, inverted or a so-called merk stave. The runes are not flat. They are multidimensional, hanging in the great Web that has no top or bottom. When you stop seeing them as flat letters and begin to experience them as crystal-like shapes, you will come to know that when they appear for you, in a reading or a casting or even as a shape seen in nature, they carry all of their wisdom, all of the time. None of it is good. None of it is bad. It just is.

There are some who issue warnings about and question the validity of the runic information that is currently being gained by individuals through personal experience and personal gnosis. They claim we must stick to the historical writings and records that are accepted within academia. What seems to have been forgotten or overlooked is the fact that all spiritual experiences, no matter when they occur, are based on personal gnosis. Past experiences are no more valid than what is being revealed to us today. If the gods and giants spoke to our ancestors in times past, why would we find it hard to believe that they are speaking to us today?

The runes are more than ancient; they are timeless. They existed long before the Vikings and long before Odin. We dishonor the runes when we view them through the lens of yet another High God. Taking them back from patriarchal distortion and hierarchical monotheism allows us to see them as they have always existed, as part of the whole that is beautifully balanced.

I have written this book and these poems from the place of my own experiences over many years. These are not endless pages of information but rather a revealing of what I have come to know and what I realize I do not know. It is my wish that my writings and my questions will somehow inspire you to listen and hear the runes for yourself.

TAKING BACK THE RUNES

We have to stop believing that deep, spiritual wisdom is only available to those who have earned it or deserve it, as if it is the exclusive right of a noble few who have suffered tremendous ordeals and trials or who have made noteworthy, ritual sacrifices of themselves.

As if there are those who deserve and those who do not.

Here it is again, the same story. A male god engaged in some special ritual that allowed him to have access to great wisdom and magic. The only way we humans can have a glimpse or get a small taste of that wisdom is through the male god.

I strongly advise you to question that story.

The wisdom carried by the runes is available to all of us if we wish to seek it out and engage with it. And rather than suffering an ordeal or enduring a tribulation, all we need to do is be quiet and listen. We do not need some special intercessor or some special password or some blood poured out by someone else, on our behalf.

The story of Odin sounds way too much like the story of Christianity, a monotheistic, patriarchal tale that includes an All Father. This should not come as a surprise. The Norse sagas were collected, translated and written down by a Catholic monk who filtered them through the distorted lens of the church.

Someone died, or suffered, or was sacrificed so we could have access to the special knowledge of life. We cannot do it on our own. Life's wisdom is guarded by some great, all-powerful keeper who withholds this wisdom from us unless we go through the right and proper channel. Oh, and by the way, the right channel always seems to be a male, and he is smarter, better, born without sin, more worthy, more deserving, than we are. You must join the special club of exclusivity.

It is time to take the runes back from Odin.
It is time to reclaim our own spiritual connections.
It is time to create our own relationships.

THE RUNES OF THE JOTNAR

The Nine

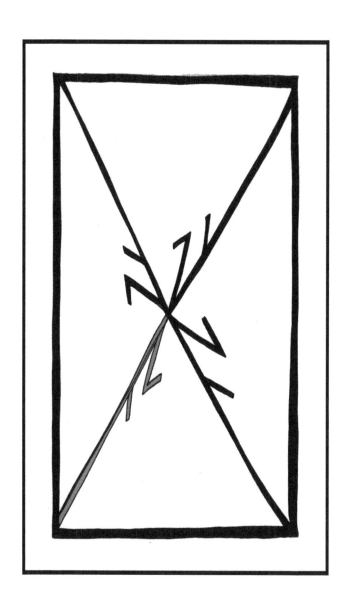

mighty Ac
lightning struck
guardian
oak of the myrkwood
nothing is as it seems
Angrboda loved trickery
impregnated
she burst open with monstrosities
birthed destruction
mothered death
who has eaten
her burned heart

AC

There is no sound more primal, more bone chilling than the howl of a wolf. The hair on the back of your neck stands on end and you pass through the veil into an ancient realm, the foreboding gloom of the Iron Wood, home of Angrboda, Chieftess of the Wolf Clan. She is howling for her children.

It was here in the undulating oak forest, muck oozing from the ground, that the shape-shifting Angrboda, skin tattooed with ink and battle scars, made love to the Trickster Loki. In their lusty, intense, all-consuming coupling, they created magic in the dark and what she birthed, she loved, but no one else did.

The high gods deceived her, luring her away from her children with a lie. They burned her until only her charred heart remained in the ashes.

Yet she lives.

Nothing is as it seems.

This is Ac.

Angrboda howls for her daughter Hela, who dragged her half-rotted corpse to the gates of Helheim to wait for her mother.

She howls for her wolf son Fenrir, cruelly chained by Odin and his cronies.

She weeps tears that mix with the waters of the ocean that surrounds Midgard, the prison home of her serpent child Jormungand.

How does it feel to give birth to children, to beings, to things that are feared, hated and despised?

How does it feel to know you have brought forth the inevitable, the chaos, destruction and death that even the gods cannot avoid?

Angrboda's heart burst and burned and yet she lives to stand beside those of us who have been cast away.

Ac is the mighty oak, thousands of years old, which stands guard at the entrance of Angrboda's home. Ac shows me the blinding flash of lightning that strikes the tree. I hear the crack as the tree splits apart and ignites, its heartwood burst open. The wisdom it reveals is the wisdom of life. Terrible monstrosities exist. The necessity of destruction must be birthed in order for life to continue.

Sometimes I ponder the question, what role does the oak tree serve when it diverts the lightning strike of Thor, the strike that would have otherwise fertilized his mother, Jord?

Sometimes I can smell the smoke and taste the charred heart.

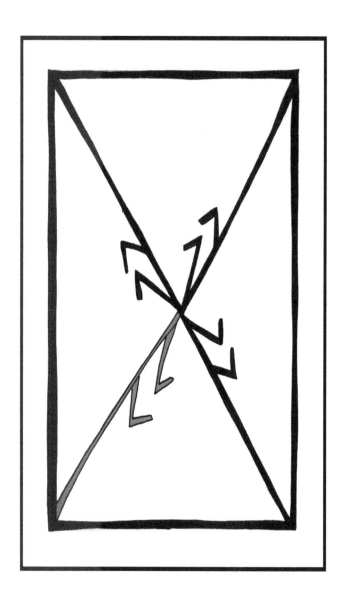

you breathe me
Os
the in and out
of all things
will you share
the poetic mead
fermented
from god spittle and blood
once
the word is spoken
it can never be returned

Os

Are you breathing or are you being breathed?
Os makes me think of such things.
When I was a little girl and I got really upset with my mother,
I would threaten her with these words, "well, then, I am
just going to hold my breath until I die."
She would smile and say, "Go ahead and try it. It never works."
I have a hunch she was speaking from her own experience.
Even if I fainted and fell over, I would start to breathe again.
Was that because my ancestors were not finished breathing
me?

Life on earth as a human, separate from your mother, begins with an in breath and ends with an out breath.

At the time of birth, does one of your ancestors decide to breathe into your new little body and inspire you?
And at the moment of your death, do you stop breathing or does your ancestor stop breathing you?

Our breath is also the way we speak.
When Os appears in a reading or shows itself in other ways, do you ever ponder the power that exists in the connection between your breath and the spoken word?
Is it true that once the word is spoken it can never be returned?
Does it take on a life of its own?

The story of the Mead of Poetry is the story of how the gods fashioned, from their own spittle, an exceedingly wise man. It is the story of how this wise man, Kvasir, came to be killed and how his blood, mixed with honey, was used to form divine mead that inspired all who drank it. And it is a story of how even more beings lost their lives because of the greed that surrounded desire. This too is Os.
Do you create with your breath and your words or do you destroy?
Do you share the poetic mead fermented from god spittle and blood?

Os speaks to me as well about the waters in an estuary.

Is the water of the river being pulled into the ocean, by the ocean, or is the river pushing its way in?

And what about the dance of turbulence and chaos that swirls around when the tidal waters rise and fall?

These questions often take me to Laguz, so I listen to that rune as well. The in and out of the tidal waters of an estuary are playing their part in the rhythm and cycles of the moon. Sometimes we do not need to push.

All we need to do is wait.

Yr
remind me
to hold focus
with silent aim
your taut bow
Skadi
releases a true flying arrow
you sustain life by taking life
the taste and smell
of blood
are your sacraments

 YR

When I look at Yr I think of the dynamic force that is present in the tension of the pulled back bow, a force that can barely be contained. I think of the stillness of aim and focus necessary to realize the intended result, hitting the target. And I am reminded that the arrow has to be pulled back before it can be shot forward. I honor as well the truth that the bow cannot be pulled back indefinitely. At some point, the tension must be released.

I see the primal force of the Uruz rune holding within itself the stillness of Isa.

Yr holds a double message.

The bow can be skillfully used to take life and the bow can be skillfully used to sustain life. Similar opposites are found in the hunter hunted aspects of Algiz.

Killing is a necessary part of life on earth. Death must always occur in order for life to continue. Here are some questions that might arrive with the arrow of Yr.

What in your life needs to be killed in order for you to live? How good is your aim?

What is your bow and what are your arrows?

Are you the skilled artisan who made them or has someone else crafted them?

Is your relationship with a tool you have made yourself different from the relationship you have with a tool crafted by another?

Skadi, the mountain giantess who loves to dwell in places where the snow never melts, embodies this rune. She can show you the way with her true flying arrow. She is a huntress and her sacrament of blood on white snow is a thing of mysterious beauty. She can be cold as ice for she stands for the laws of life that are often considered brutal or unfair but are necessary and vital.

How might you choose to honor this patroness of winter who kills in order to live?

Yr is not about hunting as a sport but rather hunting to survive and the sacredness of death. There are no places on earth where survival is not dependent upon the death of something.

What can the Yr rune teach you about life that is sustained by taking life?

How might working with the life and death energies of Skadi help you find your way?

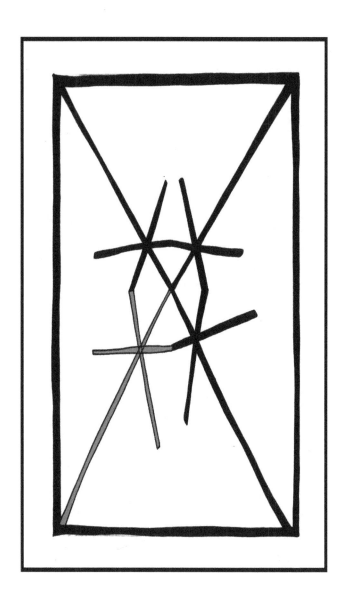

Ior
I taste you
in the salt
of my body
writhing
the gods cast you away
to avoid the inevitable
you endlessly
devour yourself
standing on the threshold
I partake of you both

IOR

Ior carries me to the salty, ever-moving, great oceans of water that encircle the globe. It opens the way for me to experience the World Serpent, Jormungand, one of the three, greatly feared and loathed, offspring of the Wolf Chieftess and the Trickster.

Ior speaks to me of borders and crossings, of ambivalence and androgyny, of single lines that demarcate and writhing, serpentine bodies that can exist on both sides at once.

Ior holds the essence of dual nature, of 'both and' and 'neither nor'.

The androgynous Jormungand thrashes and coils in the Midgard Ocean causing destruction and devastation. Its absence would cause an even greater catastrophe than its presence.

A deep relationship with Ior creates a place of balance, a place where we can learn to come to terms with the extreme and destructive forces of nature and not always fight against what is happening.

It is true that many lives are lost, not just human, and great destruction occurs in the face of hurricanes or tsunamis or violent storms at sea and we at times are saddened and stunned by the losses. However, huge upheavals on the earth, the forest fires, the earthquakes, the erupting volcanoes, are not about us, nor are they bad or evil. They just are. Sometimes daffodils bloom and gentle rain falls and sometimes, a great avalanche thunders down the mountain. The World Serpent Jormungand is daughter-son to Angrboda and Loki, sister-brother to Hela and Fenrir. The three siblings were stolen from their mother by the high gods and cast away, chained and confined. But even the great powers of order cannot hold back forever the inevitable return of chaos.

Ior can teach you how to see the curve that exists in the straight line, how to be on both sides of something simultaneously, without needing to make a choice of one over the other. Living with Ior as the ouroboros, you can come to understand what it means to devour yourself by eating your own tail. Then you can know the end and the beginning as one. This is how you partake of them both.

Working with Ior is about being willing to sail to the edge of the map, to the places you are afraid of, or the places you have been told you cannot go.
In ancient times the mapmakers drew maps of the world as they knew it, and around the edges of the maps they wrote these words.

BEYOND THIS THERE BE DRAGONS

It was believed that if you sailed to the edge of the world, you would fall off, and there you would have to face the great dragons.
Are you kept inside the realm of what is known and what is allowed, what is orderly and what is safe, by the fear of meeting the dragon when you sail off the edge?
You do not have to go there alone.
You can journey with Ior to meet Jormungand.
Sister-brother-son-daughter knows what it is like to be cast away.

hanging
on your barbed arms
Ear
I smell death
the rotting stench
there is no choice
in dire necessity
Hela welcomes all
I am inconsequential
reduced to deeds
my body feeds the earth

EAR

We all eventually hang on the barbed arms of Ear and we must all smell death, the dire necessity, the ending of life over which we have no choice.

All things live because of death. Our bodies return to the ground so they can be broken down into the elements, consumed, and then be reused to grow the food that feeds all things living.

Even those who choose to eat no flesh, eventually must come to know, that in the end, they will be eaten.

There is no rank in death. We may be remembered for

what we have done during our lifetime but in the end we are all equal. Our bodies feed the earth.

Ear is connected in this way to Othila, the rune that reminds us that the land feeds us the bones of our ancestors. Ear is often referred to as the rune of the grave and the grave never releases, it only consumes.

It is a rune of the slow process of breaking down.

It is a rune of the end result, which is also the beginning.

Ear speaks to us of Hela, she who is objective, without sentiment, she who is often considered unfair, without compassion. Her appearance, her very form, which is half alive and half, rotting flesh, reminds us that she does not hold with any kind of denial around death. Yet she is gentle and loving and will stroke your hair as you lay your head in her lap.

It is still a common practice in the United States to embalm bodies prior to burial. This is big business, a costly process that uses large quantities of toxic chemicals that eventually leak out and find their way into the ground. Embalming makes the dead body presentable, and odorless, and delays the decomposition of the corpse.

In some ways it is a form of trickery. It allows the living to imagine that the person is only sleeping, thus prolonging the denial of death.

When this rune appears it may challenge your beliefs and

attitudes around the treatment of your physical body once you die.

Does denial of the effects of death cause you to be out of harmony with Ear?

Does this denial feed your desire to retard or some how prevent the natural process of rot and decay?

Are you afraid to look at the natural face of death?

Some things that die need to be consumed by fire.
Ask Cweorth.

Some things that die need to be offered up in high places so the birds of prey can peck and tear and eat.
Ask Stan.

And some things need to be buried.

Sometimes we lay the body out on the kitchen table and attend the wake. But we leave it there, forgetting that it needs to be buried. And then we all sit down and try to eat a meal, ignoring the body.

Ear will remind you of what needs to be done.

Dig down, dig deep into the earth, below the topsoil. Bury the dead body that has been on the kitchen table way too long.

When have you been forced to offer up, to the earth, the rotting corpse that has been hanging on the barbed arms of Ear?

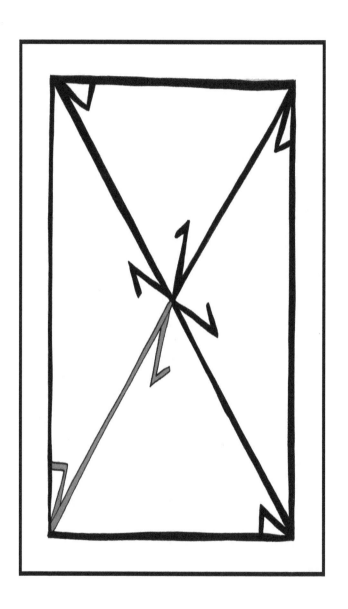

Cweorth
it is you
fire of Surt
eldest ancestor
who consumes the gods
in the end
your concern is
what must be
at Ragnarok
burn my flesh away
from bone
leaving only ash

 CWEORTH

There is an island off the southern coast of Iceland named after Surt, the fire giant of Muspelheim. Surtsey formed in a volcanic eruption that lasted from November 1963 until June 1967. It is not a tropical paradise like the volcanic Hawaiian Islands but it was formed, just as they were, by the power of Surt.

Fire from the center of the earth creates new land. Volcanoes are an inescapable part of nature. So are devastating forest fires. Amazing growth and rebirth occurs in the aftermath of both.

Cweorth is the rune of fire that changes the world. Its concern is what must be. Creation always holds hands with destruction.

In the beginning, which is also the ending, there was only the blackness of the Void and out of it appeared Muspelheim, the realm of fire and Surt, that eldest ancestor who dwells there in. His realm erupted as it collided with Niflheim, the world of ice, causing unimaginable chaos. From this chaos, new life appeared.

In 1996, another steamy explosion, in Iceland, of a volcano under a glacier, melted through 2000 feet of ice in about 24 hours. And a more recent, sub-glacial, volcanic eruption in Iceland, in 2010, sent up a 30,000-foot tall plume of ash that shutdown most airports in Europe for 6 days.

Such eruptions pale in comparison to the meeting of fire and ice in Ginnungagap. It is quite possible that the older Hela, ancestor to Angrboda's daughter of the same name, was alive at that time, together with Surt. What might she have been up to?

Perhaps we need to ask Surt what he has in mind at this time in our history as things are heating up again here on the earth.

What new creations will arise from this global warming?

To be sure, we humans have played our part in what is unfolding here, but so have the volcanoes. Perhaps Surt has taken over and is fanning the flames. He may even have a special agreement with Kari, the North Wind, an agreement we humans are not privy to.

This is the power of Cweorth, a fire so hot it burns away flesh and bone, leaving only ash.

In the end, which is also the beginning, Surt will lead the cyclical destruction of the cosmos.

It was fire in the beginning.

It will be fire in the end.

And it will be fire, in the beginning, again.

Kenaz is the fire inside.

Nauthiz is the fire brought forth from necessity.

Cweorth is the fire of what must be, destruction and creation occurring at the same time.

Do you carry any of Surt's bloodline?

It shows up in interesting places. Laufy knows. She gave birth to Loki. He carries the bloodline of his fire-giant father, Farbauti. Sometimes the bloodline is quite evident in humans who are glass blowers, fire fighters or blacksmiths.

In the end the gods will be consumed.

In the end Surt will remain.

In the end there will be fire because fire cannot be destroyed.

There are some things in life that need to be buried, offered up to the earth where they are slowly broken down and used.

There are some things in life that need to be burned, quickly consumed, smoke rising up, leaving only a pile of ash.

When you develop a relationship with Cweorth, as well as the rune Ear, you will learn to know the difference between earth grave and funeral pyre.

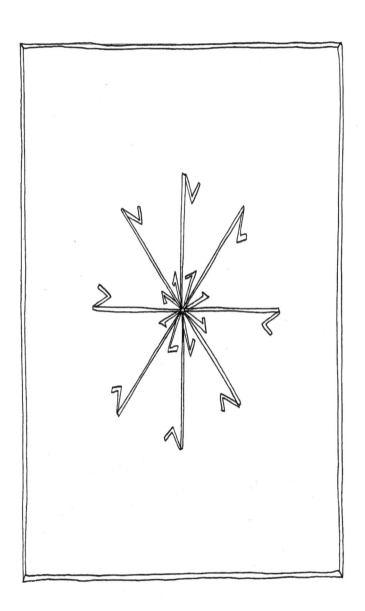

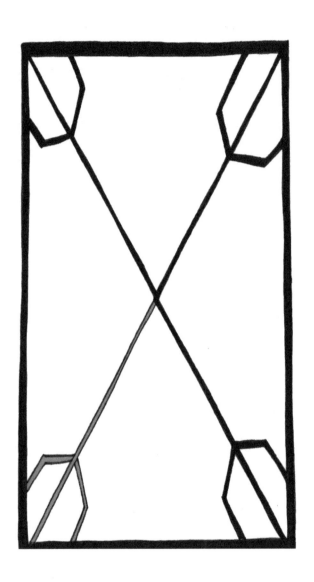

Calc
I hail thee
raising the mead cup
the gilded horn
I pour out my offerings
to the gods
honoring memory
chalk turns to bone
earth to blood
you provide
nourishment
for Yggdrasil

ᚲᛅᛚᚲ

I stand on the mound pouring out an offering to the gods, an offering given in exchange. This is an endless cycle. The cup holds many things when it is full to overflowing. Do you partake of it all or do you partake of some and then pour out the rest?

Sigyn's cup catches and holds the venom, caustic and punishing, that drips on Loki. Even the smallest droplets burn her hands and when she leaves for only a moment to empty it, Loki writhes in pain.

There are bowls that hold the Mead of Poetry that was made from honey and the blood of Kvasir, the wise one who was formed by the gods from chewed berries and communal spittle.

There is the Cauldron of Aegir where the beer for the gods is brewed.

There are containers that hold the blood of warriors and containers that carry the blood of sacrifices.

There is the gilded, aurochs horn filled with fermented liquid, carried by Freya, she who receives the dead into her hall, Sessrumnir, found on the field of Folkvangr. It is from this gilded horn we all must drink in the sacred marriage of death.

What are the contents of your mead cup?

Who holds it for you?

Or do you carry it yourself?

And when it is full, do you drink from it before you pour it out?

Or are the contents something other than liquid?

The skeletal remains of ancient sea creatures, compressed by the weight of ages, form chalk and chalk is used to fertilize the earth where the crops grow. We are fed by the crops. We are blood and bone and we return, ultimately, to the ancient seas that nurture the sea creatures that become chalk. We must pour out so we can drink.

Memory is a powerful thing. Without it we do not know who we are. To remember is to honor. To honor is to offer something up.

Looking at Calc you might see, instead of the upturned container, the three roots of the World Tree, Yggdrasil. Others do. Each of the three roots grows into a different well.

> Urdarbrunnr
> Hvergelmir
> Mimisbrunnr

At some time in the far distant past, did Calc contain something valuable and sacred that was poured out into the wells, that water the roots, that water the tree?
And if so, what was it?
And where did it come from?
And did it also fill your cup?
Pouring something onto the ground nourishes the ancestors.
How do you honor your ancestors?
How do you honor their memory?
How do you feed Yggdrasil, the World Tree?
What are you willing to pour out when Calc appears among the runes?

Stan
you are the bones of Ymir
killed by kin
you guard
entombed eagles
buried in rock cairns
petrified by salted wind
I stand
by megaliths
unmovable
I wait for them
to open

 STAN

I love Stan. It is solid and closed and reminds me of large rocks and boulders and standing stones. Stan feels like family. I am related, in part, to a long, ancestral line of imps who often made their homes in the windswept, rocky landscape of Northern Scotland.

Stan carries me back thousands of years to chambered, rock cairns, to Stone Age tombs, to places such as Isbister, Tomb of the Eagles, in the Orkneys. In these barren, isolated hills in the north of Scotland, human bones and artifacts have been found, secreted away in tombs, piled together with the bones of white-tailed sea eagles, the eagles with the sunlit eyes. Stan causes me to wonder what part these giant birds of prey played in the lives of my people.

Were they sacred totems or powerful protectors who were interred with the ancestors to guard them in the afterlife? Were they connected somehow to the excarnation process, the tearing away of the flesh from the bones of the laid-out bodies?

The rocks remember. If we lean up against them, lay our bodies on them, they will open to us and speak.

I had an amazing experience in Ireland in the spring of 2014 at Kernanstown Cromlech, County Carlow, also known as the Brownshill Dolmen. This burial chamber that dates back almost 6000 years has a capstone still in place that is estimated to weigh 100 metric tons. It is believed to be the heaviest capstone in Europe. The chamber has never been excavated so it still holds all its secrets. These enormous stones, pitted with age, covered in lichen, and dripping with damp, asked me to lay my body onto them so I could listen to them speak.

I have often wondered how ancient people managed to move megaliths over long distances and put them into place. This is what the stones told me, that cold, rainy day in Ireland.

"You trouble over much and miss the obvious. We

are the living offspring of Ymir, who was killed and dismembered by his grandson Odin. We moved ourselves to this location, just like all the other large stones have moved themselves. We were sacred to your people. They communed with us and used our energy and power to support their lives. We have chosen to stay here in these forms, as keepers of the memories of all that has happened on this land and all that has happened to its people. Some of us have grown weary and have fallen over. Some of us have been split apart and damaged. Some of us have been desecrated. We are family to the mountain giant Mimir. He has been standing so long, guarding the Sacred Well of Memory, he has grown into the mountain just like we have grown into the landscape. We are living stones. We will open to you when you are ready."

What could you learn from Stan by being willing to lay your body up against a boulder and listen?
What would the living stone tell you?
Would it tell you if it was a barrier or a guardian?
Would it open to you as a portal or would it be an unmovable megalith?
What relationship do you have with the Jotnar, the giant elemental beings from the beginning of time?

Gar
gift of Ing
you are the one
who brought them forth
tore a hole
in Ginnungagap
runes
rushed in and out
with piercing wail
the high one
sacrificed himself
ending the beginning

ᚸᚪᚱ

For some, Gar is the ending rune. For others, it is the beginning. For the runes, it is both. The circle is continuous, unbroken.

The question is, where did you enter the circle?

The runes existed, shimmering and vibrating, in Ginnungagap long before Odin grabbed a handful of them from the Well.

The runes do not belong to Odin. They are not his, nor are they his to give.

It is time to take them back, that handful of runes and return them to the whole.

Rather than looking at Odin's actions as something favorable, why not shift perspective? What if his actions were about entitlement?

> "I am going to do this great sacrificial thing and then I have the right to take some of the runes and claim them for myself."

Rather than believing Odin did us a favor, why not consider the possibility that the scream came because he tore a hole in the Gap when he wrenched the runes from the Web?

If rune wisdom is universal wisdom that has always existed, is it not available to all of us? Why would we need a god to make a sacrifice?

Is this not just another 'we should be so grateful we need to be saved' story?

Always working with the runes in reference to Odin dishonors them and in fact limits our ability to form and develop relationship with them ourselves.

The commonly accepted belief is that Gar represents Odin's spear, the one he used to stab himself in his sacrificial ordeal.

But I ask, what was the wisdom of Gar before Odin?

One of the ways I see Gar is as the beautiful pattern that is formed when the two runes Gebo and Ingwaz are bound together. I call it the Gift of Ing. It is very sexual in nature, the shape of the Ingwaz rune being the vaginal portal or opening, with the Gebo rune placed on top. The slightest pressure on the center causes the four lines of Gebo to fold up toward each other, making it possible for Gebo to pass through the Ingwaz rune to the other side. The offering, the gift, passing through the opening of fertility.

Gar is one of the most complex of rune shapes. When you look at it closely you can see that there are five Ingwaz runes held within it, four small and one large.

I have runes tattooed on my arms. I have Gar tattooed on the back of my left hand, right next to the dragon. Gar asked me one night to be silent and still so it could show me something. What I saw was how the god Ingvi Freyr was brought, long ago, to the British Isles by the Germanic tribes and how they worshiped and honored him each year by pulling him around the countryside, in a wagon, in a circuit that was formed by the shape of Gar. The rune pattern was superimposed over the entire island in such a way that it mirrored a star pattern that was present in the night sky at certain times of the year.

As the wagon and the people followed the circuit, they would stop and perform rituals at each point where the lines of the Gar rune intersected Ingwaz. Standing stones marked these intersections. The rituals activated the blessing of Ingvi Freyr and insured the fertility of the land.

What can be seen in the dark and heard in the silence when the handful of runes that Odin grabbed are returned to the whole and the tear is mended?

WHAT HAPPENED TO AUDHUMBLA

Audhumbla was a cow. She came from Ginnungagap, emerging from the chaos, when fire embraced ice, forming freezing fog and frost rime. She appeared at the same time that the amorphous Ymir came on the scene.

The fact that this cow was lactating indicates she had recently given birth.

The fact that she nursed Ymir from her teats tells me she had just given birth to this giant being. And the fact that she licked the ice tells me she was not bovine.

No, Audhumbla was a reindeer cow.

Runes are so much older than the domestication of cattle. Long before our Northern European ancestors even thought about keeping cattle, they had close association with the reindeer.

So what happened to Audhumbla?

She disappeared just as suddenly as she appeared. Somehow she was written out of the Norse stories of creation and the focus was placed instead on the males, Buri, Bor and ultimately Odin. Somehow, it seems to have been forgotten that Audhumbla freed Buri from the ice and that Ymir was fed from her milk-filled udder. As if writing her out of the story would make it easier to convince us that life comes from the male.

Does this not seem like a story we have heard before?

A story of absence.

A different twist on the tale might be to bring Audhumbla

back into the story, and consider that this lactating reindeer cow, who emerged from the darkness of the Void, was
the beginning.

She.

Not he.

Maybe it would be more truthful to call her All Mother
instead of calling Odin All Father.

How might your relationship with the runes be affected if
you returned Audhumbla to the story?

This might well be the (un) familiar journey with the
runes.

We would stop viewing them simply through the lens of
male-dominant, warrior cultures such as the Vikings.

We would not confine them to the time frame of agrarian
cultures, people harvesting grain and domesticating cattle.

We would no longer speak of them as belonging to a
so-called High God who is inappropriately called All Father.

We would read against the grain the writings of a Catholic
monk who lived in the early twelve hundreds and we
would look for missing clues about the females that have
been hidden under the oppression of the patriarchy.

And we would ask, what happened to the cow?

On this journey we would stop viewing the runes as a

mere secular alphabet, or worse yet, simplistic markings to use in video games.

We would not try to turn them into some form of Tarot or speak of them in the language of New Age, white light, pop psychology.

We would honor them instead and in so doing we would honor our ancestors by remembering.

THE RUNES OF THE ELDER FUTHARK

The First Aett

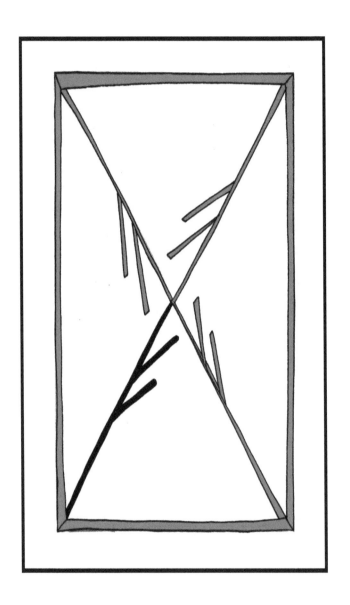

it is you Fehu
the spark
manifested
at the beginning
all wealth
arising from the land
Ymir suckling
Audhumbla licking ice
fearing mortality
I hoard
hinder
withhold
possessed
by possessions
I am consumed

FEHU

Fehu takes me to the place of remembering. All wealth
arises from the land and the land is the earth and the earth
is the mother and it is the mother who gives birth. So
everything comes from her, even money, and developing a
relationship with money is developing a relationship with
the earth and the mother.

Have you ever thought about money that way?

The earth gives birth to money just as she gives birth to all other things. It is energy coming into form.

In some of the old myths, the mother gives birth to the son, who in turn becomes her lover. He pours himself out, impregnating her and then dies. She ripens and produces another son, who in turn becomes her lover.

If we can imagine becoming the mother of money, then we can imagine giving birth to it. Once we do that, we make love to it by using it. This causes it to die. But it leaves us full and impregnated so we can give birth again. This is how money is spiritual.

Life emerges from the Void and then returns, over and over again. Order emerges from chaos and then returns. The moment we forget this, our lives quickly lose their balance. This loss of balance will often show up in the relationship we have with our possessions.

It is not about being rich or poor.

It is not about whether we own a little or a lot.

It is about how we view what we have.

It is about how we hang on.

It is about energy coming into material form. When we hoard we are out of balance.

When we accumulate belongings we do not need or use, we are out of balance.

When we have possessions we are afraid to let go of or get rid of, we are out of balance.

When we choose to live a life with very few personal possessions but somehow carry the energy or belief that we are better or more spiritual because of this, we are out of balance.

When we have just enough to barely get by. so we are always struggling and constricted, we are out of balance.

When we are possessed by our possessions, they eventually consume us.

There is a certain climate evident in some spiritual communities that promotes the belief that money and wealth are somehow undesirable. This belief seems to carry with it a great deal of judgment.

Have you ever heard any one say,

> "I don't want to be rich, all I want is to have just enough to get by."

You may have even said those words yourself.

If material things are just energy that has come into form, then the same holds true for money. It is just energy in form.

Who would ever say,

> "I don't want a lot of energy. All I need is just enough to get by, just enough energy to make it

through the day, doing what must be done, so I
can drag my exhausted body into bed at night,
too tired to even sleep, only to get up the following morning and do the same thing again."

Why would anyone say such things about money or energy?
Take a look at nature. There are great examples of abun-
dance and opulence and even what appears to be excess.
How many blossoms does an apple tree really need?
How many apples?
The truth is, it only takes one apple to keep the whole
thing going. A new apple tree can grow from a single seed
and there are several seeds in a single apple.
What about sperm? It only takes one to fertilize an egg.
And how many eggs does a fish really need to lay? Nothing
goes to waste. Nothing is too much. All energy is used and
reused, over and over again. All money. All wealth.

I often think of the energy of Fehu as it relates to self-
storage units.
We fill up our drawers.
We fill up our cupboards.
We fill up our closets.
We fill up our garages.
We overflow and we fill up our storage units. There are
currently about 60,000 self-storage facilities in the
United States, which amounts to more than 2.35 billion
square feet of storage. The individual units come in all

sizes, some as small as a walk-in closet and some as large as a two-car garage.

There is an enormous amount of stuff being stored, ranging from junk to heirlooms. People pay money every month, sometimes large amounts of money, to store stuff they do not need. If they needed it, they would be using it, not storing it. Year after year they keep paying. Sometimes people pay for so long they forget what they are storing. Just imagine how much energy is bound up in all these possessions.

What could happen if all that energy was released?

How could the money being spent on storage be redirected?

How might the space be used differently?

Just imagine some of the things that could happen if all the storage-unit space was freed up and all the money redirected.

What if storage units were used to house the homeless?

What if the money we spend on storing stuff was spent instead on providing homeless people with food and clothing?

That would cause a tremendous shift in energy.

Are you possessed by your possessions?

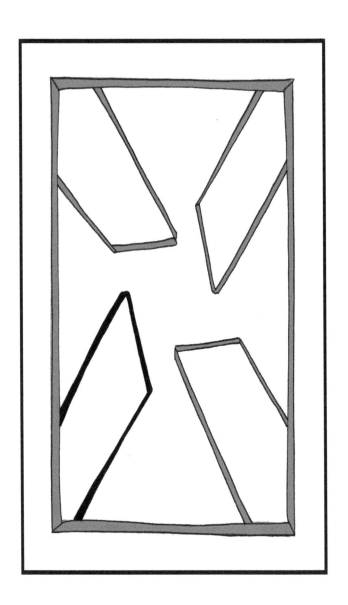

I drink to you
mighty aurochs
fearless
formidable
Uruz
it takes courage
to honor a foe
I search for you
in the animal
of my own body
tamed and civilized
I face extinction

URUZ

Life is wild, nature is wild, and we are wild. Creativity
comes from the place of wildness. And we do not have to
be in the wilderness in order to be wild.

Uruz carries the very essence of wildness. When we are
always trying to tame the wilderness, civilize the savages,
control and manipulate nature, when we lose our connection to the earth, the elements, the seasons and cycles of
life, when we deny or demonize our bodies, our sexuality,

our fecundity, we create such an imbalance in life we actually face extinction.

Being domesticated and civilized often means playing it safe, living life in a way that is acceptable, predictable, conforming. I compare it to the life of a milk cow that stands in front of the dairy barn. She is safe, she is fed, but she is being milked to death. In order to keep producing milk she has to be bred over and over again and as soon as she gives birth, her calf is taken away so she will not bond with it. Perhaps it is safe and predictable to be a milk cow, but there is a huge price to pay.

Do you ever feel like you are being milked to death?

What would it be like to take your chances and be wild and free?

When Uruz appears in a rune reading it often carries with it the question, where in your life have you sacrificed your freedom and your wildness in order to feel safe and be accepted?

It asks that you take a long hard look at your life and tell the truth.

Uruz can easily be identified with the mighty aurochs, an enormously grand species of wild cattle that once inhabited Europe and the northern reaches of Scotland. The aurochs actually survived into the mid-sixteen hundreds, which means it passed into extinction not so very long ago.

There are some spiritual practices that actually discourage wildness, either by implying, or stating outright, that spirit is more holy than flesh, that we must transcend our bodies, and aspire to states of high vibration that take us away from the earth and all its beauty. There are spiritual practices that teach that there is something wrong with the earth and being human, that we are only here to learn lessons before moving on to something better. Interestingly, these supposed lessons seem to come to us only through pain and suffering.

Do you live somehow disconnected from the earth because you believe you are from someplace else and you are always trying to get back to wherever you think you came from?

Try instead to come back into harmonious alignment with the wild, free, creative, sexual energy of Uruz and avoid the extinction of your amazingly glorious human self.

Ifing the river is called
I will cross over
the bridge
impregnated
by your hammer
expectant
in the storm
you torment and fester
until chaos
births fertility
Thurisaz
my firstborn
belongs to you

THURISAZ

There is a river that separates the realm of the gods from
the land of the giants. Ifing the river is called. Ifing, the
River of Doubt.
It runs so swiftly ice never forms on it.
It runs so swiftly it is difficult to cross.
Why does there need to be a separation between the gods
and the giants?
Why would this separation be called Doubt?

And how is it that Thor crosses over the river so easily?
He most definitely carries the blood of giants from his mother's line. She is Jord, giantess of earth and soil, land and crops, and the daughter of Nott, the giantess of Night. Thor most often gets placed in the Aesir pantheon along side his father Odin but rarely does anyone remember that Thor is more than half giant. So is Odin for that matter. And they both cross over the river into other realms.

Thor is a storm god much loved and honored by the people. He is roaring thunder and flashes of lightning that strike the earth and fertilize the soil. His hammer is used in the blessing rituals of new brides, imparting fertility. His hammer is hung on the plow as it turns the soil in spring, thus assuring abundant crops for the coming year.

When Thor arrives in the storm, in his chariot drawn by goats, does he use his hammer to impregnate his mother? Is this yet another story of the mother who gives birth to a son who becomes her lover?

The frost giants are called Thurs, so perhaps Thurisaz is the rune of these giants. They appeared at the very beginning out of the chaos of fire and ice.
Does Thurisaz carry with it some of the chaos that exists at the moment of emerging?
When it shows itself in your life or in a reading, it would serve you well to ponder.
What is my river of doubt?
Which side of the river am I on?

Where am I the most comfortable?

How easy is it for me to cross over?

What impregnates me and when I give birth, who claims my firstborn?

Do I deny or ignore the parts of myself that carry the lineage of the giants of chaos?

Do I favor instead only the parts that the high gods approve?

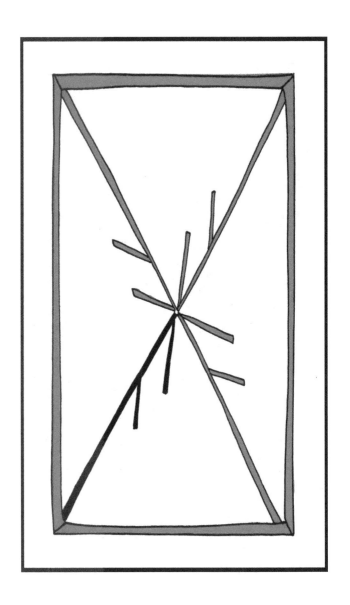

through you
Ansuz
through the spellsong
a sacrifice screaming
I was spoken into existence
runes poured forth
woven
unbroken
ancestral lines
twisted
by breath and wind
I am the container
I am contained

ANSUZ

I dance with Ansuz in my relationship with words. Words are alive and have an existence separate and distinct from the way we so often, mindlessly, use them. They are creations in and of themselves. They have a generative power. True, they may limit us when we use them to describe what we experience or how we feel but at the same time, they have the power to change our perceptions as well as create them.

The psychologist James Hillman wrote about 'the ange-lology' of words. The word angel originally meant an emissary or a messenger and the Ansuz rune helps me remember the value and significance of the messages that words carry.

Each word and each rune is a personal presence with its own gender, history, mythology and genealogy.

Words and runes are about voice and sounds.

How do you use your voice?

It is not a matter of whether you speak. It is a matter of whether or not you use your voice to speak about things of value, and whether you use your voice to speak of things with integrity and truth.

We compromise our relationship with Ansuz when we engage in gossip, idle and unconscious speech, and lying. And once we are out of balance with Ansuz we become out of balance with our breath, because breath is the means by which we speak. And breath is about life.

We no longer live in an oral culture so a good question to ask might be whether or not Ansuz can connect to our writing voice as well as our speaking voice.

Ansuz is about air. Just like fish live in water, we humans live in air. It is easy to forget about air because air is invisible. We may enter a room and say that it is empty because we do not see anything in it but the room is not empty. The air is there, so the room is full and the air is always full, full of things seen and unseen.

Air is all around us and air is inside of us. We are the container. We are contained.

Ansuz also connects us to the ash tree, sometimes called the honey tree because it secretes a sugary substance from its bark and leaves. This honey from the ash tree, when fermented, has hallucinogenic effects on those who consume it. Called the Mead of the Gods, it opens up the way for us not only to have communion with the gods but also to speak in their voices. There was, and perhaps still is, a custom in the Scottish Highlands where mothers use the tip of their finger to feed their newborn infants the fermented sap of the ash tree, thus linking the child to the gods from the moment of their birth.

How might things be different if we still followed such practices today?

The presence of Ansuz may cause you to question your thoughts and beliefs about the use of hallucinogenic substances in rituals.

Can they, do they, connect you with the gods and the power of creation inherent in words?

Do the gods of the air breathe into us each time we take an in breath?

And if that is the case, is the air we expel when we speak, the spirit, breath and voice of the gods?

Whose breath mingled with Odin's breath when he saw the runes, grabbed them up and screamed?

Is that what is meant by a sacrifice of self to self?

What is spoken into existence at the time of sacrifice?

Ansuz might lead you to Saga, the Norse goddess of poetry, she who creates history by reciting the stories of ancestral lines. Daily she drinks the sacred mead.

Ansuz might lead you to Bragi, the Norse god of poetry and eloquence who is said to have had the runes carved on his tongue. Poetry carries the magical power of words. It can touch our hearts, stir up memory and longing, as well as inspire. It allows us to partake of the realm of the gods through the use of words. It was, and still can be, used as a memory aid to keep the ancient stories alive. Poetry allows us to take hold of the woven, unbroken, ancestral lines that are constantly being twisted by breath and wind.

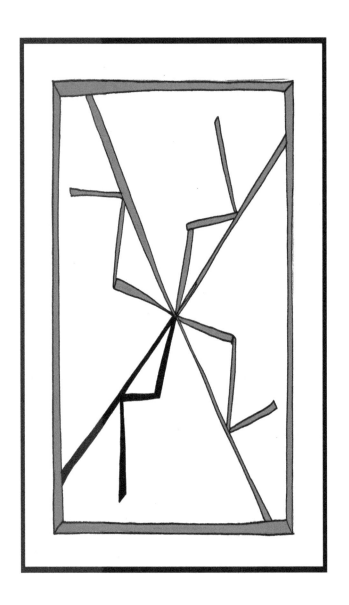

Raido
the adventurer
is on the move
drum and hoof
Odin mounted
moving between worlds
all things change
remain the same
I ride my future
into the past
someone
comes to meet me

RAIDO

The beat of a drum. The pounding of horses' hooves.
Rhythmic movement and sound.
Are you riding or are you being ridden?
Raido is a rune that thunders in, heavy with questions.
Can you call upon Raido when you desire movement or
change to occur?
Is it possible to be in motion without actually moving?
Can change occur without things actually changing?

Can you channel the power of movement, according to your will, to produce the results you desire?

How does being at the right place, at the right time, doing the right thing carry the power of Raido?

Is it possible to be at the wrong place at the wrong time and be doing the right thing?

What do you believe about the concept of right and wrong?

Is the rune about controlled and orderly movement, such as the sun and moon across the sky?

Can there be order and control in movement even when it does not appear to be so?

If you carry the runes with you when you travel, does that mean that the rune of travel is traveling?

How does travel affect you?

Can you travel without actually going any place?

Have you ever considered that all travel might be a spiritual experience?

What really happens as you move through time and space, through geographies, climates, cultures, and languages?

It is easy to see Raido's energy in objects being moved or moving but what about the movement that takes place on the inside?

The fluids within your body move even when you are still. So do your cells.

When you see a tree branch moving do you assume it is being moved by the wind or is it possible that the branch is moving itself?

This question is similar to the one I asked about breath and the Ansuz rune.

Are you breathing or are you being breathed?

Odin is said to have ridden his eight-legged horse between the worlds.

Can we do the same using Raido?

The horse was sacred to many of the Norse and Germanic tribes. Horse-worshiping cults practiced rituals such as sacrificing horses, partaking of their flesh, and even mummifying body parts, such the penis, and using them in ritualistic ceremonies.

Can we connect with the wisdom of Raido by using its energy in a sexual way?

In his book *The Spell Of The Sensuous*, David Abram raises questions regarding the possibility that the past as well as the future exist just beyond the horizon, that place in the landscape where the perceivable joins that which is present, but cannot be seen.

Using this question, we can explore the possibility that we can literally walk our way into the future, which lies beyond the horizon, and we can just as easily turn around and walk our way back, into the past.

When you do that, do you meet yourself?

This is the mystery and power held in Raido, riding our futures into the past.

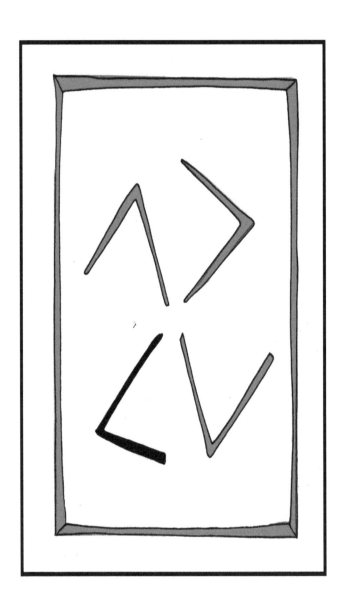

remembering
more than blood
my ancestors
were etched inside
Kenaz
split me open
I penetrated the darkness
I saw what was destroyed
spun and woven
frayed and worn
the strands of Wyrd
retied

KENAZ

There is a difference between knowing things because we
have studied them and knowing things because we are born
knowing them. This knowing is more than intuition. It is
the wisdom of the ancestors that lives inside each and every
one of us, in our blood and in our bones and in our cells. If
we are willing and allow it, Kenaz can split us open so we
can see and understand these things we already know and
remember the wisdom we were born with.

born to it

Kenaz shows us how to see in the dark without using our literal eyes, without the need of light. There are some who say the rune is attached to the concept of light and illumination and refer to it as the pine torch but the use of the words light and illumination might limit our understanding. Light is only needed to see when we are using our literal eyes. Kenaz opens things up so we can see without eyes and see without light.

When you form a relationship with Kenaz you will begin to have a sense that you are remembering things that you knew long ago. This is the power of the rune. Kenaz activates the inborn, hereditary knowledge that comes to us from our ancestors. So whenever the rune appears, the ancestors are using it to open us up so we can connect with them. But we have to be willing. It can be like an initiation into a sacred place. Kenaz initiates you so you can access the wisdom that you carry inside yourself. The shape of the rune is a wedge. Using a wedge makes it easier to split things open. It intensifies the force of the axe when chopping wood. You can use Kenaz to split things open so you can more quickly and easily understand. It can open up the way for you to go into the dark, hidden, and unseen places and see without needing light.

Are you caught somehow in the belief that you always need to be enlightened in order to know?

Have you forgotten how to use Kenaz to see in the dark?

There are two ancient rune poems that connect Kenaz to ulcers and rotting flesh.

If I sense that the rune's appearance in a reading has something to do with health, I will ask the question, does this illness come from being disconnected from your inner knowing or your inner wisdom?

If you close your eyes and let Kenaz split you open what do you imagine you will see?

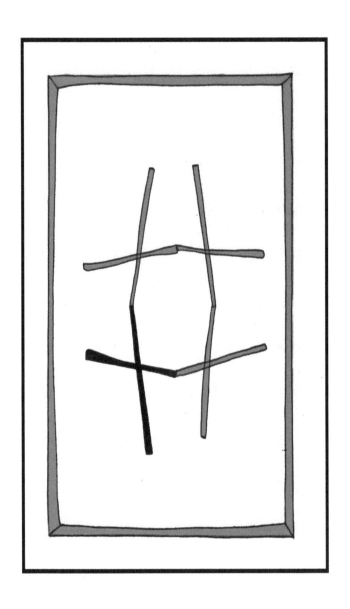

Gebo
all gifts and obligations
carry your presence
the runes
the gods
demand of me
a sacrifice
what I pledge
binds me
releases me
all gain requires loss
all life is equal exchange

GEBO

It is a lie that there is more happiness in giving than there is in receiving. One cannot exist without the other and because of that, they are equal.

Whenever you hear someone parrot the phrase, 'there is more happiness in giving', it might be valuable to stop and ask the question who is benefiting from such a belief?

The Gebo rune holds within itself the energy of equal

exchange, both the giving and the receiving. For the ancient people of the runes, the act of giving was considered to be noble and highly meaningful. Hospitality often meant the difference between life and death for the traveler or the wanderer. Not only did hospitality need to be extended, it needed to be accepted as well. The acceptance was as binding as the giving. Both acted as a pledge.

The essence of Gebo also offers us a great reminder that not everything that is offered in the form of a gift, is actually a gift. Take a look around your own life and see how this might be true.

Have you ever been given a gift that you really did not like, did not want, did not need and would never use?

Do you still have it?

Why?

Are you being held hostage by the hook that was embedded in the gift?

 "I can't get rid of it. My mother-in-law gave it to me and she would be devastated."

"My brother would really have his feelings hurt if I didn't keep this."

"My best friend carried this all the way from (fill in the blank) in her suitcase and I would never dare to tell her I hate the color."

Such examples might seem trivial but they are examples of instances where the energy of Gebo is out of balance. If you feel obligated to keep something, then it was not a gift.

And what about the times when you are the giver? I worked with a woman once where the presence of Gebo in the reading had to do with the caretaking she was giving to her brother who had cancer. She had moved in with him in order to provide care but she was really angry. When we got down to the root of the matter, she was angry because he was unwilling to do things, regarding his health and possible recovery, in the way she thought was best.

What Gebo helped to reveal was that her gift of caretaking was conditional. There was no doubt she was giving out of love but there was a part of the caretaking that was not being given freely. It had a hook. It was the part that held the expectation of how he was supposed to behave. It was really hard for her to admit this, but she had to become clear about it herself in order to know how to do things differently.

The Teiwaz rune that was also present in the reading, asked her to speak the truth, first to herself.

Would she take care of her brother only if he behaved a certain way, or would she take care of him no matter what his choices were?

Telling the truth to herself allowed her to remove the hook from the gift.

 Gain is not possible without loss. Every decision requires that you release something simultaneously as you accept something. This is the power that exists in giving and receiving.

Does it bind you?

Are you obligated by it?

The giving of a gift can also present a challenge. Hierarchy, status and pride can be bound up in the giving, as well as in the gift itself.

Galina Krasskova, ancestor worker, priest of Odin and Loki, cautions that a gift is a dangerous thing. It always demands a price, the energy involved in paying and the energy involved in receiving.

What are your thoughts on this?

Gebo will speak to you when you decide to work with the runes. It will ask you what sacrifices you are willing to make in exchange for the wisdom you seek?

Wunjo
fulfiller of wishes
you care not
for wisdom or folly
you lead me
both to joy
and madness
in death
in the presence of the gods
in sun filled halls
I drink

WUNJO

Wunjo is often called the rune of joy perhaps the joy of
perfection, or bliss.
It can be associated with ecstasy, and madness as well,
giving rise to the questions, are there different kinds of joy
or is joy just joy?
Are there differences between states of joy and states of
ecstasy and madness?
Can we come into relationship or alignment with Wunjo
through the use of sacred plant medicines, things like mush-
rooms and fermented tree saps or perhaps even drugs?

Can we connect to Wunjo through states of ecstasy or bliss attained by dancing, drumming, fasting, or even sex?

Would some of these methods be deemed more spiritual, more sacred than others, and if so why?

Joy can come from blessings and abundance.

It can be experienced alone and it can be experienced as part of a family, clan or tribe. The joy that comes from being in family or in community brings along with it expectations and obligations that are not there when you are alone.

I often find in readings that the lack of joy a person expresses is tightly woven together with their unwillingness to accept the accountability and responsibility that go hand in hand with the joy that comes from being part of a family or community.

What are your own experiences with this concept and the Wunjo rune?

Have you ever struggled with your desire to experience joy as part of a relationship, with an individual or a group, and your unwillingness to accept the responsibility that goes along with it?

Wunjo can connect us with the joy of the Otherworld or Afterworld. To the ancient Norse, the world after death was considered a place of great joy. The halls where the dead ate and drank were filled with light, and it was from these places the dead were able to give attention to the well-being of their kin and clan.

Have you ever connected joy with the dead or your relationship with them as your ancestors?

Wunjo also reminds us that even the smallest movement of air can bring a storm.

As I am writing this, I am sitting outside in Portland, Oregon. It is a summer evening almost 9:00 and a breeze is blowing. I am reminded of Wunjo and its shape. It looks like a small, triangular flag at the top of a flagpole. Even the slightest breeze will cause the flag to flutter. Even the slightest breeze will cause a change in the weather.

When you feel Wunjo move, even if it is almost imperceptible, do you consider that there might be a change coming in the weather or climate of your life?

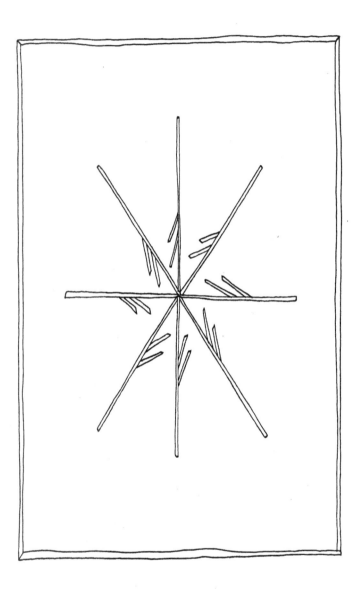

THE RUNES OF THE ELDER FUTHARK

The Second Aett

most holy of runes
fearsome stormbringer
the gods provided
signs and portents
greater than the realm of man
I ignored the warnings
bound in Helheim
by Hagalaz
Hela
braids and unbraids
my hair

HAGALAZ

We are all affected by storms in nature. They are bigger and more powerful than we are. It is not possible for us to predict them, much less control them.

I often experience Hagalaz as the rune of Hela. She is the Storm Bringer, the Destroyer. She is one of the forces that moves through nature wild and untamed. Dragging her half-corpse self through the worlds she spreads fear and dread, as do her siblings, Jormungand the world serpent and Fenrir the ravening wolf. These children of Angrboda and Loki are anything but loved. But there is a gentle, caring side to Hela. She knows what it feels like to be cast away. You can rest your head in her lap, finding comfort there, as she cradles you with her arm of flesh and strokes your hair with her skeletal hand.

Have you been bound too soon in Helheim, the realm of the dead, because you did not pay attention to the signs? Did you not see the storms coming?
Do you imagine you can ignore them and carry on with life as usual?
Do you insist on chopping wood or riding your bicycle in a hailstorm or do you wisely seek cover, knowing it will quickly pass?

Hela the Storm Bringer causes thunder and lightning, whirlwinds and hail, just by combing her hair, binding and unbinding, braiding and unbraiding. Her connection with hailstorms binds her to Hagalaz.
The fear of the power held in a woman's hair is ancient and this fear is still evident in spiritual practices where women are required to cover their hair and in religious orders where women are required to either shave their heads or cut their hair short.
I wonder sometimes why it is so common, so popular, for older women in Western culture to cut their hair short. In fact, it is often encouraged, supported by claims that short hair makes a woman look more youthful.

Does it really?

What if the underlying reason for cutting off a woman's hair is more about how powerful she is when it is long?

Would you be so willing to cut your hair short if you knew that it held great power?

Would you be so willing to cut your hair short if you knew that in some unspoken, subtle way, it represented giving in to the control and manipulation of male-dominant, patriarchal systems?

In Germany there still exists the old custom of baking special bread at winter solstice and giving it as an offering to Frau Holla or Hela, Mother of the Dead. This bread is braided and called Holla's Zopf.

What ancient wisdom regarding death is bound up in the braiding of hair?

Northern Tradition shaman, Raven Kaldera, reminds us that it is all or nothing with Hela and the Hagalaz rune. It is not enough to walk away. We must forget who we are and be willing to say, I have no name.

Pay attention to the signs and portents.

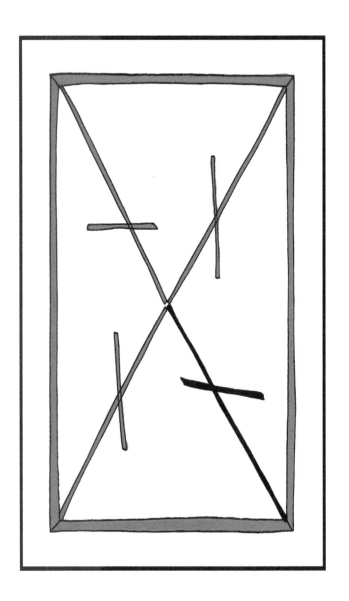

summoned by need
gaunt from starvation
I emerge
slowly from the cave
Nauthiz
you are a hungry rune
fueled by bitter necessity
fierce with determination
your friction
sparks ancestral memory
ancient fires ignite

NAUTHIZ

Do you resist resistance?

If you are trying to start a fire by rubbing two sticks together or by using what is called a bow drill, you cannot oil the sticks. Not everything in life is about flow and ease and the law of attraction. Some of the great things in life require friction, resistance, persistence and determined effort.

What follows is a story I often tell when Nauthiz appears in a reading.

It is cold, dark, damp and you are hungry. You need to build a fire and all you have is the bow drill, a primitive wooden tool used to create the spark that is needed to start the fire.

You have a need.

You have an intention.

You have a tool.

You are determined to persist until you start a fire. But what you also need is friction and resistance. Without them the wood will never heat up enough to create the spark. This is not the time to oil the wood. You would oil the wooden hub of a wagon wheel to keep it from catching on fire but never the wood used with a bow drill. This is not the time for frictionless movement or ease. Rather, it is a situation that calls for effort, resistance and persistence. If you resist the resistance, or stop too soon, your need will not be satisfied.

There is something else you must remember. Once the fire starts, you do not need to keep rubbing the sticks together.

Fire is alive and each individual fire that comes into being is an offspring of Surt, the great Fire Jotun of Muspelheim.

In your efforts to make fire of any sort, do you ever think to call upon the gods or do you just take things for granted and assume fire will always be there for you?

Many of us in the modern world have lost our connection with the sacredness of fire. All we need to do is strike a match, flick a lighter, flip a switch, turn a knob or press a button.

How different would your relationship with fire be if your very life depended upon starting one and the only way to start one was to know how to do it yourself?

Would you call upon the great fire giants to assist you?

Would you take for granted that you could do it alone, without their help?

Would you show appreciation?

The Nauthiz rune asks all of these questions.

Nauthiz is a hungry rune. It can only be satisfied when the need is met and the solution exists in the need.

It is a sexual rune.

The desire, the friction, the passion, the necessity to reproduce. Sex is part of our hunger for life.

It is a creative rune.

The urge, the longing, the effort, the potential. Creativity is the need to make something new.

Nauthiz binds us to our ancestors and their need to have fire in order to live. It binds us to the giants of fire, to Muspelheim, and hence to creation. It reminds us that our spirituality cannot be only in the mind. We cannot transcend the physical or material but rather we must use our bodies to participate in the necessity of life.

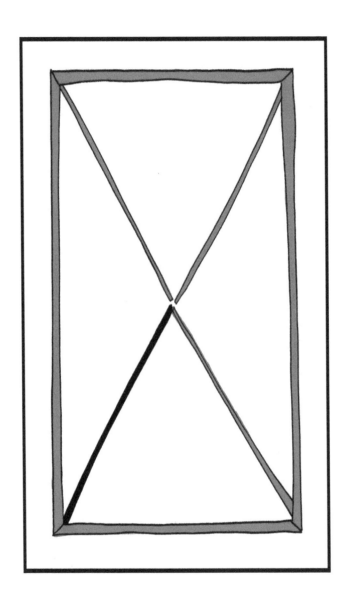

Isa
realm of ice
home to all the runes
the crushing weight of ages
you float
hissing
groaning
there is movement
in your stillness
preservation in destruction
enthralled or released
I serve you

ISA

The first time I realized that Isa was home to all the runes,
I was drumming. I saw her lying on her side, a single hor-
izontal line and when I looked closer I realized she was
not a single line, she was layers of lines, one on top of the
other, like the layers of ice that form on a glacier, year after
year after year. And I could read what was layered there by
lifting off the single lines and reassembling them back into
rune shapes.
When I was shown this, I was told that as the ice is melting

runes are being released and revealed. We have been limited in our understanding of and relationship with the runes because we have only focused on small groups of them, like the 24 that make up the Elder Futhark or the other nine referred to as the Anglo Northumbrian runes. Rune staves are the signatures of powerful, energetic beings who are guardians of universal truth and they are unable to be numbered.

One of the creation stories of the Northern European tribes tells us that, in the beginning, fire and ice came together in the great void. And out of that chaos, life emerged.
What grand, watery creation is taking place right now, on earth, as the fire is melting the ice?

Ice is a great preserver as well as a destroyer. We put things, such as meat, into the freezer as a way to preserve them. If we leave meat in the freezer for too long, it will ultimately become ruined.
Freezing is a way to slow down the movement of water but there is still movement. The nature of water is to move.
What can you learn from Isa about the movement that exists in stillness?
What have you frozen in order to preserve it?
Has it reached the point where it has been frozen too long?

Could you use the wisdom of Isa to know when it is time to thaw something out?

Isa holds within herself the wisdom of changing form as well as the deception that is possible within appearances. When water freezes it becomes solid, thus creating a bridge, a way to cross over. But even though it is solid, it may not be strong enough to carry any weight.
Dazzling in the sunlight, it can be treacherous and slippery. And as it is with black ice, you may not even know it is there. One of the most fascinating aspects of ice, for me, is that it is solid but rather than being heavy, it floats.

Isa, home to all the runes, I am enthralled. I am released.

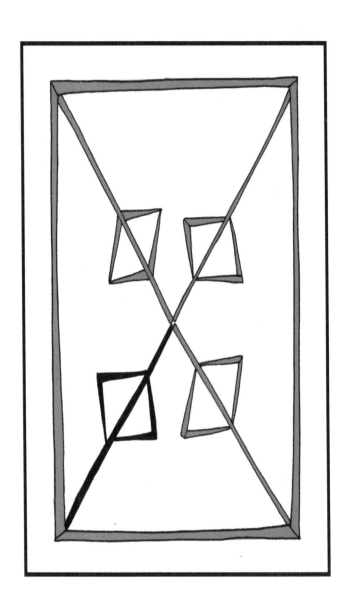

the wheel turns
Jera reaps
threshes
the golden hair of Sif
I must learn
to rest and labor
with the seasons
I cannot rush
I cannot delay
life
comes from death
at harvest

JERA

Jera's appearance always seems to say, it is time. The wheel of the seasons has turned. Winter is approaching. An apple has fallen from the tree. The nuts need to be gathered. Jera carries the wisdom that is present in the earth, in the autumn, at the time of harvest, the wisdom that reminds us that ripening cannot be rushed, nor can rot be delayed. Once the growth cycle is complete, the process of decay begins.

growth or decay

We are not separate from nature. What happens in nature happens to us as well.

Harvest is a time of discernment, of paying attention, to life, to the seasons, to circumstances. You have tilled the soil, planted, watered, weeded and waited. You are ready to gather in nature's bounty but there are things in life over which you have no control.

It does not matter how much you wish for something to happen. It does not matter how positive your thoughts are or how much effort you put in or how much worrying you do. Sometimes, nothing grows or what has grown is diseased or defective, unfit to harvest. Sometimes, things must be left in the fields to rot, decay and return to the earth. Winter never comes early, Spring never comes late. It may seem otherwise to us when we try to compare what is happening in the present moment to past personal experiences or to memories of how things have been before. Nature has its own wisdom and rhythm and Jera reminds us that the wheel turns at its own pace. It is part of a cycle we may not understand and over which we have no control. We all must learn to value rest and labor, growth and decay, gain and loss, life and death, the opposites held within the wisdom of the turning.

Jera reminds us of the truth that if barley is planted, barley is what will grow. So do not be surprised or disappointed. If you do not like barley, do not plant it. Plant something else. If that is all you planted and that is all that has grown, oh well, you may have to eat it or go hungry. And next time, plant something different.

Jera reminds us, as well, that all things have their own timing and cycle. If you plant onions, they sprout rather quickly in the spring and are soon ready to eat. The same is true with lettuce or radishes. But if you plant an oak tree it can take 20 to 30 years before it produces acorns.

Jera teaches us about discernment, the ability to distinguish and discriminate. Not all things should be harvested. Some crops need to be left in the field. And during the winter, no matter how long it is, we dare not eat everything. That is short sighted and dangerous as well. Some seeds, grains, and roots need to be stored away, untouched, so they can be used in spring to replant and reseed.

How do these principles apply in your daily life?

What are you trying to rush?

What are you hoping to delay?

What needs to be left in the field to rot?

Where do you need to practice more discernment in order to make it through the winter and still have something left to use in spring?

Sif is a Norse goddess closely associated with the rune Jera. She was a consort to Thor, a thunder giant. According to the myth, Loki, who is often called the Trickster, cut off the golden hair of Sif, goddess of grain. Supposedly, Sif felt great shame because her hair was shorn. Thor was angry and demanded that Loki replace it. Loki commissioned some dwarves to fashion replacement hair from forged gold and as the story goes, Thor was well pleased.

What might be the significance of a story such as this?

Was Sif's hair grain?

Was it time for it to be harvested?

If so, why was there an issue over it being cut?

If power truly exists in a woman's hair, did Loki somehow take away her power when he cut it, causing Sif to feel shame? In nature, if the grain is harvested at the right time, its power is not lost. It is held in the kernel, which when planted, grows again. Life comes from death at harvest.

So why would Thor be satisfied with replacement hair fashioned, by dwarves, from gold?

How could the male gods imagine that they could quickly and easily replace what the earth naturally provides and consider it to be superior as well?

How could something growing from the earth be replaced with something forged from metal?

Does this version of the story of Sif somehow support the belief that the gods can replace the goddesses?

Does Jera carry a lesson for our times?

How often do men place more value on the things they

invent, manufacture and produce than they do on what grows naturally from the earth?

How many of us have lost our connection to Sif because we have moved away from the land?

How many of us have lost touch with the vibration of Jera?

Do you consume food that is forced to ripen by the use of toxic, ethylene gas?

Do you eat food that is forced to grow by the use of poisonous, artificial fertilizers?

Do you buy food that is not native to the climate in which you live or is out of season and needs to be flown into your area on jet planes?

Is the food you eat overly processed, commercially manufactured or unrecognizable?

What choices do you make to stay in balance and harmony with Sif and Jera?

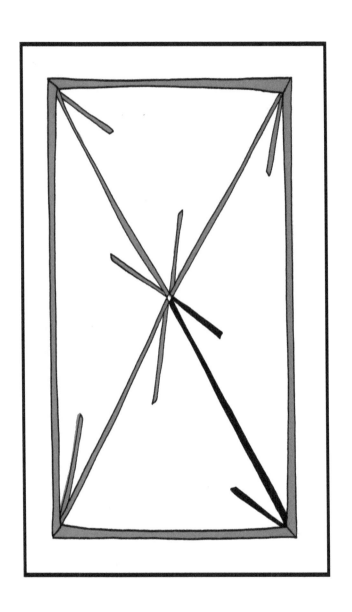

I come to see
Eihwaz
sacred yew of life
growing
from death
singing
songs of renewal
who will I become
through willing sacrifice
self to self
fearing the end
I forget to live

EIHWAZ

It is said that yew trees grow out of the mouths of the dead buried in the cemetery. Perhaps that is so. It is common to find very ancient yews growing in churchyards and some of them have grown out of the graves. Since they live for thousands of years, it seems likely, as well, that the graveyard was formed around the trees. Invading Christians loved to claim for themselves the sacred hills and groves that were revered by the people of the land they were conquering. The ancient yew groves were places where sacred rituals were held, the mysteries of sex, birth and death, places where you could go to be altered by the mildly hallucinogenic, resinous vapors that are released from the yews.

No yew tree should ever be considered dead. The remains of rotting trunks can be thousands of years old and then suddenly come to life again. A great deal of energy is held in the branches that grow down and root themselves into the earth. This makes it possible for the tree to grow again by sending up a new shoot from inside a hollow trunk. The yew tree grows again and again from its own rotted-out corpse.
We all grow from the corpse.

There are some who say that Odin hung himself on the World Tree, Yggdrasil, and their argument is that Ygg is one of Odin's names and drasil is an Old Norse word for horse. Perhaps he did. We must remember however, that the World Tree was there in the Void from the beginning, which is also the middle, which is also the end, and all of that was there long before Odin came on the scene.
So what was the name of the tree before it was called Odin's horse?
We might have forgotten but the Jotnar know.
Some say the World Tree is an ash and some say the World

Tree is a yew. And some might even say that the World Tree is every tree and all trees.

What do you say?

If you know it as the yew then you may know its connection with Eihwaz, often called the rune of life and death. If you know Eihwaz as the rune of the World Tree you may also know it as the rune that will assist you in traveling to the Nine Worlds that exist in its roots. And you will know that the branches and the roots mirror each other.

Eihwaz is the trunk with the branches growing up and the roots growing down.

Eihwaz is the branches growing down to become roots that send up a trunk that grows new branches.

To know this rune is to sit with your back up against a tree trunk and feel the life energy of the tree become mingled with the life energy of your body.

Death is born in the middle of life and a relentless desire to stay eternally youthful, to pretend we are not aging, is imagining we can avoid the second half of life. Fearing the end we forget to live. Eihwaz is a relentless reminder that no one can stop the turning of the Great Wheel.

Eihwaz can be experienced as a rune of initiation.

Are you willing to die to yourself so you can become something new?

Have you ever worked with the Eihwaz rune in this way?

When you come into a close relationship with it, you will be asked to reevaluate your beliefs about the concepts of down and up, below and above, lower and upper, bottom and top.

Do you believe that the branches are superior to the roots? Do you believe that what is above is good or more important that what is below?

What would happen if we turned the tree upside down, turned it just like the Eihwaz rune turns? Then we could see that there is no difference. Those who dwell above are not somehow better than those who dwell below.

The Eihwaz rune reminds us that there is no top or bottom, there is no above or below. There is only constant motion. This is true of the earth as well. It has no top or bottom. It just hangs in space, constantly moving.

Eihwaz reminds us that there is no seen and unseen. All things are visible. We limit ourselves when we think we can only see with our physical eyes.

Eihwaz will ask us to examine the beliefs we hold regarding the shamanic realms.

Is there really a separation?

When we speak about upper, middle and lower realms and the beings and the gods we imagine dwell there, do we place a value judgment on the different locations?

When we decide to place the gods, spirits, and creatures in the upper, middle or lower regions, do we hold to the belief that they must stay there or that they always reside there?

Who are we as humans to determine that?

Is there a hierarchy present in who or what we decide to place where?

Have you forgotten how to live in wholeness because of how you view above and below, higher and lower?

Are you willing to hang upside down, in sacrifice, in order to have a different perspective?

What is your song of renewal?

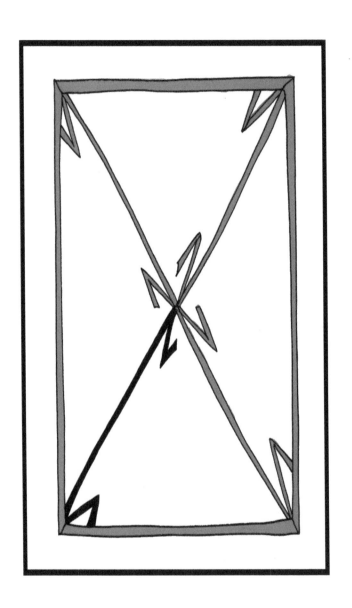

Pertho
you are the pouch
guarded
by the Norns
a womb holding secrets
a woman
crouching
in childbirth
the gods demand both
play and sacrifice
taking me down
to the roots and well

 PERTHO

The night is moonless and cold. The fires are lit in the
hearth of the great hall. Straw and reeds are strewn on the
floor and dogs wander about looking for scraps of
food. The long, heavy benches are drawn up alongside the
scarred and worn oak tables. The game board is laid
out. You have your pieces and I have mine. We each know
the rules. You can sit there and ponder, strategize, calcu-
late and project, even imagine what it is you think I will

do, what move I will make, but at some point you must step into the realm of the unknown.

You must reach into the pouch, gather up the dice and roll them.

You must take action.

You must be willing to play the game.

You make your move, so that I can make mine. And then, only then, will you know what other moves to make as you watch the game unfold.

This is life and so we begin.

Pertho is the rune of chance, of birth and beginnings, of something coming forth from the pouch that is known as well as unknown.

Look at her shape. She is the woman crouching in child-birth. She is the pouch that holds the dice that are rolled in the game of life.

The things that are known are the board, the pieces, and the rules. The thing that is not known is the roll of the dice. But we cannot just wait for the unknown to be revealed. We must participate in the play.

Spirituality is not just about being serious. It is inseparably linked to our creativity, our sexuality, and our willingness to play.

The gods want us to join them in the great halls, noisy, loud, and boisterous, with all the smells and tastes and the sights and sounds of life. They want us to play with them,

knowing that there are no guarantees, no assurances, of
what the roll of the dice will unfold or reveal or how the
pieces will be moved.

Our spirituality must be playful and risk-taking, and human.
It is detrimental to our well-being to get caught in pious,
trite sayings, such as, 'it must be your karma', or 'you must
have chosen this thing so you could learn a lesson', or 'it
was meant to be', or even worse, 'it was God's will'.

I always wonder why it is that these supposed lessons we
have to learn are always delivered to us in the form of
suffering or pain, struggle or loss.

Can it just be the roll of the dice?

Have you ever heard anyone say 'it must be a lesson you
are supposed to learn' when things go really well for you
or your life is incredibly wonderful and successful?

Our lives are not just a predetermined set of events? No,
we play the game of life with the gods and it is our willingness and participation with them that determines and
changes the outcome over and over again. Yes, there are
threads of Wyrd that have been spun and woven before we
came into existence but we get to spin and weave our own
threads into this tapestry, thus creating our own patterns.
For me, this is Pertho, the rune of chance. This is the rune
that reminds me of the Nornir. It is she, Urd, Verdandi and
Skuld, who sits by the Well in the roots of the World
Tree. She was there before the gods. She knows what
cannot be changed and she knows what can. Even the

gods must consult with her prior to handing out decisions or decrees.

I follow Pertho down into the dark, into the earth, into the roots of the Tree.
I follow Pertho down into the Well, to the waters that hold the ancient wisdom of the runes.
I follow Pertho down to learn what I need to know about my willingness to roll the dice and to take a chance.

It is she who plays with you as you roll the dice with the gods, in the mead hall, on those dark, winter nights, when the dogs doze, warming themselves in front of the fire.
Are you willing to roll the dice?
Are you willing to play?
The gods demand both play and sacrifice.
Let Pertho take you down to the roots and Well.

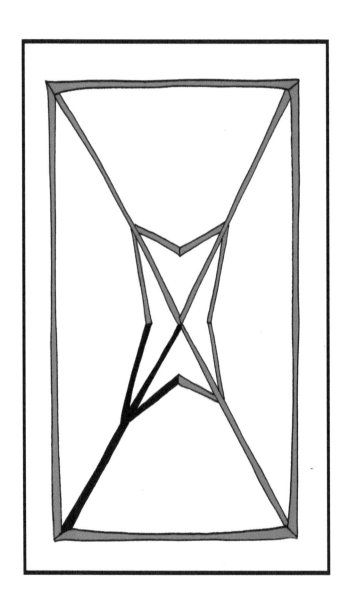

Algiz
of the antlers
tine before the eyes
embodied
in my upraised arms
I ask
am I the hunter or the hunted
in danger and protected
I follow the herds
across the ice

ALGIZ

There is danger in concealment. Most of us do not think about that. We more often think of hiding as being a way to be safe or protected. But it is always about perspective, is it not. It depends on whether you are the hunter or the hunted. This dynamic seems to show up quite often in rune readings where Algiz appears.

Here is a story I tell.
The stag hides in the brush or undergrowth, unseen by the hunter, but it cannot stay there indefinitely. At some point it must get up to find water and to feed. So it stands up in

all its glory, head held high. The hunter may still be there and then again, he may not. There is a risk indeed but that must be weighed against the guaranteed outcome of staying hidden, eventual death from thirst and starvation.

Where in your life have you hidden, perhaps to keep safe or to go unnoticed?

What is going to happen to you if you stay there and do not risk standing up in all your glory, arms raised, so you embody Algiz?

Is it time?

My experiences with Algiz often take me to the reindeer. They have, what I call in the rune poem, a tine before the eyes. A tine is an end point of an antler. In reindeer, it is compressed into a shovel shape that protrudes from the brow line, usually on the left side. They use it to dig in the snow to find food.

Humans have followed the migrating herds of reindeer since the beginning of time. When the weather changes, reindeer turn and walk into the wind, into the direction of the storm. They migrate to find food and they migrate to find safe places to give birth. The Sami people say there is much to be learned by looking at life through the eyes of the reindeer.

When the Algiz rune appears it might be a good time to question which way the wind is blowing in your own life.

If you follow the reindeer, where might they lead you to be fed and to give birth?

There is also great sexual energy present in Algiz, as the Kenaz rune moves up and down the Isa rune and the Isa moves in and out of the wedge.

Can you feel it?

Reindeer.

Male and female.

They both wear the mighty antlers.

I rise at dawn
to greet you Sunna
singing your song
Sowelo
you grant sight
you blind the arrogant
wolf chased
horse drawn
you disappear
again
I rise at dawn
to greet you

SOWELO

When was the last time you got up early enough to watch
the sun rise?
Have you ever sung to her at dawn?
How do you experience the sun?
As male or as female?
Some of the Northern European tribes spoke about the
sun as being female. They called her Sunna, the bringer of
life and light, warmth and new growth. Sunna melted the
ice of winter. She was pulled across the sky each day in a

chariot drawn by horses, Alsvith, whose name means All Swift and Arvak, whose name means Early Waker. She was chased by the wolf Skoll who sometimes came so close he took a bite out of her.

Our ancestors in the north had a relationship with the sun that was different from the people who came to conquer, a relationship different from the armies of Rome and the monotheistic priests who brought with them a religion born in the desert. Desert people do not know the midnight sun, the sun that shines through the long summer nights when the sky never darkens. Desert people do not know the sun, the sun that never rises up in the sky through the long, cold winters.
Northern European sun celebrations, at winter and summer solstices, carried great significance and meaning. They truly marked the coming of the darkness and the returning of the light.

We are living in an interesting time, a time when we smear our bodies and our children's bodies with chemicals and then spend long hours in direct sunlight, imagining we will not suffer any ill effects just because our skin does not burn. We believe we can override our body's natural warning system and suffer no harm. We do not really know the extent of damage being caused by the sunscreen or the prolonged exposure.

We shield our eyes from the sun by filtering her light through dark glass, forgetting that it is vital to our health and well-being for the full spectrum of her light to enter our bodies through our eyes. What parts of sunlight are you missing when you wear sunglasses?

Has it just become a habit?

How might it be affecting your health?

There was a time when people honored the sun. This is no longer true. Now she is treated more like an enemy.

We have forgotten her sacred symbols and we have forgotten her fair name. We have forgotten her rituals and her songs. And there are very few of us who remember to welcome her back at winter solstice. Most people are so focused on the supposed birthday of a male child, son to a sky god, they forget to honor the real birth, the return of the sun.

How is it that in our search for enlightenment we have forgotten to honor the sun?

How is it that in our arrogance we have forgotten that she who gives us light can also blind us?

What makes us so sure that the sun will rise every morning or that she will return at Winter Solstice?

Before the advent of clocks, people knew what time it was by knowing where the sun was in the sky or in relationship to features of the landscape. You would have to live in a place a long time to learn where the sun would be at a certain time of day, at a certain time of year. Knowing time this way is very different from knowing time that is arbitrarily determined by clocks, time that does not relate to anything, time such as Daylight Savings Time.

Forming a relationship with Sowelo can strengthen your relationship with the sun and that will shift your relationship with time.

Do you ever wonder where Sunna goes at night?

Does she disappear into the earth?

Does she sink down into the ocean?

What do you see at sunset?

Who takes care of her and guards her while she is away?

Have you ever dared to follow?

Have you ever asked her in the morning where she has been all night?

Or why she stays away longer in the winter than she does in the summer?

When the Sowelo rune comes to you, what questions might you ask about the sun?

THE RUNES OF THE ELDER FUTHARK

The Third Aett

can there be justice
in lies
I ask of Tyr
order over chaos
is loss always present
in compromise
strength of convictions
demands a price
who dares deny
the wolf
his true nature

TEIWAZ

Can there be justice in lies? Teiwaz shows up again and
again in so many readings and in so many conversations.
What happens when we really tell the truth?
So often I hear people say they cannot be truthful because
it would hurt someone's feelings or upset someone or that
their partner, family member, friend, work associate just
would not understand. If you are currently living your life
from the place of fear and compromise then perhaps
Teiwaz can point the way back to integrity.
Loss is always involved in compromise.

Strength of convictions always demands a price. Integrity begins with telling the truth to your self.

This is the story of Tyr and the wolf Fenrir, son of the giantess Angrboda and Loki, brother to the great serpent Jormungand and brother to Hela who dwells in the realm of the dead.

This is a story most often told from the perspective of Tyr, a warrior for truth and justice, who upholds the traditional sources of authority. In the popular version of the story, Tyr is a hero because he keeps chaos at bay and loses his hand to the wolf in the bargain.

There is another part of this story that is rarely explored. Tyr lost his hand because he lied to the wolf and tricked him into being bound with the magical chains that the dwarves had made.

Why did he do it?

Why would he lie?

Because the high gods told him to?

Because he was afraid to go against traditional sources of authority?

Because he believed it was necessary to keep the peace?

No matter the reason, Tyr suffered a loss when he compromised his role as a truth teller.

No doubt he would have paid a price as well if he had

gone against the orders of the other gods and refused to lie to the wolf. But the price would have been different from the loss suffered because of compromise.

And what about the wolf?

Do we ever hear the story from the perspective of the wolf or in support of the wolf?

A wolf is a wolf is a wolf. It is the wolf's nature. Of course he bit off the hand of Tyr.

What else would a wolf have done in the face of lies and treachery?

Working with the spirit and essence of Teiwaz gives you the opportunity to dig around in your own issues of truth, compromise, integrity and loss.

When you reflect on the story you can ask yourself, who am I in the tale?

Am I the high gods, the wolf, Tyr?

Am I perhaps the hand that got eaten?

There is no right answer.

There is no wrong answer.

Only you can say what is true for you.

Here is one of the many things that happen when you do not speak truth to those around you. First, you justify your withholding. You say something to the effect that speaking truthfully would cause upset or anger or conflict. Your withholding creates an energy that is ever so subtle but can still be felt by the other person, even if they are not aware of what they are feeling. They have an animal sense that something is off, not quite right and that creates the energy of distrust. They pull back from you and withhold because they sense you cannot be trusted. Once they do that, you feel it, and then you feel justified and right in the decision you made to not speak your truth. And then it just builds from there. All this happens on an almost imperceptible level. It can happen in a matter of seconds, or over a long period of time. It is not so much about what you say but rather what you do not say.

You can call upon Teiwaz to support you in living with integrity and strength of conviction, enjoying relationships based on truth telling and trust.
You can ask yourself, where in my life am I compromising myself, my dreams, my health and happiness because I am afraid to go against the high gods, or have been convinced it is my duty to keep the order at the expense of my own truth?

Teiwaz can support you in building a strong sense of self-worth so you fearlessly live your true nature.

I am warned
the devouring mother
discards as well as nurtures
she who births
also destroys
when I poison you
Berkana
you feed me
death in return
beware
this is the mystery
life

 BERKANA

To watch the arrival of spring after a long, cold winter is
to know the magic of Berkana.

To watch a mother dog push a runt from the litter and
refuse to feed it is to know the wisdom of Berkana.

So often emphasis is placed only on the nurturing, protec-
tive, care-giving aspects of the Berkana rune. We must
never forget that there is always balance in the mother's
wisdom. It is expressed in her knowing what to nurture
and what to cull, what to feed and what to kill. She

destroys, ignores or pushes away things that are defective, weak, sickly, or unable to thrive.

Such actions do not need to be considered negative or bad. They are just part of the whole, the balance of Berkana.

The runes are not moral, nor are they judgmental. They are keepers of universal wisdom and such wisdom demands that some things in life need to be destroyed early on or allowed to die on their own. And some things that are birthed or brought forth need to be nourished and protected. Believing that only some of the activities of the mother are good creates a dangerous imbalance.

The law of life is that the mother births and nurtures, and she devours and destroys.

She knows she must care for herself first in order to care for others.

She knows that if she is fed poison she gives back poison in return.

Where in your life do you care for others at your own expense? Even the most loving mother will have her milk dry up if she does not take care of her own needs as a priority over those of her nursing baby.

What in your life needs to be discarded, pushed away or left on its own?

Who feeds off your energy when it is not appropriate?

Where in your life are you still breastfeeding teenagers or suckling adults?

These can be hard questions to ask your self.
Answering them can help you align with the wisdom of
Berkana.

As I am writing this, the skies over most of Oregon, California and Washington are filled with the thick smoke of
forest fires. It is the summer of 2015.
I am reminded of the Norwegian Rune Poem for Berkana.

> *Birch has the greenest leaves of any shrub*
> *Loki was fortunate in his deceit.*

At first it might seem a bit strange that Loki is mentioned
in the poem. Loki is a trickster figure in Norse myth, with
prolific reproduction being one of his primary characteristics. He was born from the giantess Laufey after the fiery
arrows of Farbauti struck her. Laufey's name means Tree
Island. The Berkana rune's connection with the birch tree
carries a theme of the rebirth and return of life to the
woodlands and forests at the end of winter as well as after
the devastation of fire. And even though Loki's actions are
dangerous to the gods and to humans as well, they are
nonetheless necessary for new growth to occur.
Thank you Loki for the necessary but difficult devastation
of fire.
Thank you Berkana for wisdom to both nurture and destroy.

sacred horse
saddled
you carry the gods
to their greatness
the dangler knows
rhythm and movement
mastery and surrender
riding your energies
Ehwaz
I set boundaries
while crossing them
I become my equal

 EHWAZ

The bond between horses and humans is ancient and runs deep. We rode them. We worshiped them. We ate them. In fact, clear up until the twelfth century, heathen Swedes were called horse eaters. For tens of thousands of years humans have hunted and eaten horses. Some of the oldest cave paintings ever discovered show scenes of ritual hunting of horses.

The horse was a sacred creature that carried the gods on adventures and exploits, pulled chariots across the sky and was worshiped and used in ritual and fertility practices by many ancient European tribes. There were horse cults where the King mated with a sacred mare to insure the blessing of the realm. Horse penises were preserved or mummified and used as sacred objects to promote or bless fertility. It is no surprise then that Odin, who rides between the worlds on the eight-legged horse, Sleipner, goes by the name of Volsi, Horse Penis, which can also be translated The Dangler.

In some cultures it is believed that centaurs came into being when the sacred horse penis mated with mother earth.

Who are these magical creatures?

The imagery of the centaur is found even among the stone carvings of the Picts, an ancient tribe of northern Scotland.

Our ancestors knew that sexuality, spirituality and creativity were bound together in life and that riding these energies allowed them to move between the worlds.

How far can you ride the energies of Ehwaz?

What boundaries could you cross?

What realms of greatness are you willing to explore to become equal to yourself?

Ehwaz is the rune of horse and horses, of horse and rider, of freedom and control, mastery and surrender. You cannot ride a horse by pulling back on the reins any more than you can drive a car with one foot on the break and the other on the gas.

Often in a reading, Ehwaz will ask the question, where in your life are you bound, harnessed or yoked to someone or something that is not your equal?

Do not be fooled. Both a pony and a draft horse can pull a cart or wagon to market. But they cannot do it if they are bound together. They will only go in circles.

They can walk the same road, in the same direction.

They can walk the road with the same intention. But they must do it separately.

So ask yourself, where in my life am I bound to someone or something that is not my equal?

Where in my life am I going in circles?

Who in my life do I need to disconnect myself from in order to move forward?

Ehwaz may show up when there is something great and powerful trying to move you and move through you. Movement is both creative and destructive. Movement can be both frightening and exciting.

Set the fear and uncertainty aside, relax the reins, and become one with Ehwaz and ride it.

all the holy races
stand connected
at the bridge
where have I separated joy
my sex
from the gods
my body
from the divine
Ask and Embla
join together
Mannaz
breathes as one

 MANNAZ

We live in a world that is not just about us, was not created just for us, a world that can and might very well continue on, without us. It is a world that is more-than-human. Everything is unique and everything is special but nothing is more important than anything else. We humans do not hold some superior place any more than the gods do. There is no line that divides the gods from the humans, or the humans from the rest of the world. We are all sourced from the darkness of the Void.

This is our home. We are not aliens here. We live entirely

within the great realm of all things. There is no place to go and there is no place we have come from. Such imaginings cause a sense of hierarchy and separation. When people talk about being from the stars or from other galaxies, it is often in that rather hushed tone of specialness.

I smile and say,

> "That's great! Then we must be related. I'm from the stars too, because I'm from the earth and in case you haven't noticed, it hangs right in the middle of the cosmos, surrounded by stars."

All things existed in the Void and the Void was there from the beginning, and the beginning is also the ending, because it is a cycle, a circle, a repeat.
That is how all the holy races stand connected at the bridge. That is how Mannaz breathes as one.
We come from the great Void, Ginnungagap, and the chaos caused by the coming together of Niflheim and Muspelheim.
We come from that famed tree Yggdrasil in whose roots exist all Nine Worlds.
We come from Audhumbla, the reindeer cow that birthed and suckled the giant Ymir.
We come from the places that were formed from the parts of Ymir's dismembered body.
We come from the wood the gods found on the sandy shore and then used to form Ask and Embla.

We come from Heimdall who fathered the social order of men and who guards the Bifrost Bridge.

And we are all joined together as one because we all come from the Void. We must face and touch each other just as the two Wunjo runes do when they form Mannaz. This is the doubling of the joy, to recognize the connection.

It has become quite common and popular to speak about the runes using pretentious New Age jargon. They are often compared to the Akashic Records, Buddhist Enlightenment, Christ Consciousness and the Higher Self. And so much that is written about Mannaz focuses only on the mind. There are several online, rune-study communities that speak about Mannaz using words such as evolved, perfected, transcended, and self-actualized. The runes stand alone. They are sentient, independent beings who do not need to be compared to other traditions or ideologies.

The spirit of Mannaz teaches us what it means to be a human and humanness is not just about the mind and intellect. We cannot separate our minds from our beautiful, perfect human bodies, from the magic and messiness of our sex and sexuality, from our cravings for food and pleasure, from our connection to the earth.

When we value the spiritual over the physical we separate ourselves from the joy.

An underlying sense of dissatisfaction, depression and discontent is fed by the belief that there is always something wrong with being human, that we are only here to learn some lesson on our way to enlightenment, or ascension, as if there is someplace to go, as if there is someplace better or more real.

Our physical bodies are not sinful and imperfect, corrupt and defective. We do not need to shed them so we can evolve, ascend or become divinely enlightened.

Mannaz connects us to our wholeness as humans, our sexuality, our spirituality, our creativity and our perfection.

Who are you when you stand connected at the bridge?

you are lake and well
stream and fen
the waters of my own body
shape shifting
Laguz
deceptive
destructive
life giving
I dare not judge
all rivers flow
the ocean refuses no one

LAGUZ

Laguz is about water and our relationship with water, the water on the earth and the water in our bodies. And a relationship with water is not possible unless we have an intimacy with the moon as well.

Our lives are the waters of Laguz. We begin life in the water of our mother's womb. We come forth from that water at birth. We lived in water once, but as soon as we are birthed from it, we can no longer live in it. And yet, it is impossible for us to live without it.

As an element, water can exist as liquid, gas or solid. It takes the shape of the container it is in. Because of its natural ability to dissolve things, it rarely exists in a pure form. Laguz is a shape-shifting rune.

More than seventy percent of the surface of the earth is covered with water. More than sixty percent of our body's weight is water.

The gravitational pull of the moon, as it revolves around the earth, is so powerful it creates a visible bulge on the surface of the oceans. It lifts the water up out of the ocean and then releases it, creating low tides and high tides. A pull as powerful as that most certainly pulls on the water in our bodies as well.

Knowing where the moon is plays a vital role in understanding our emotions and how we feel. A relationship with Laguz and water must include a relationship with our bodies and the moon.

Many interpretations of Laguz connect it only with the soft and gentle, flowing, feminine energies of water but to get caught up in such one-sided thinking is to be deceived. It is true that water is all of those things and it is also just as true that water is raging, destructive, and powerful enough to gouge out the Grand Canyon and wash away entire cities.

A one-sided perspective of Laguz dishonors its elemental potency. Water is gentle and it is destructive. Water is life giving and it kills. Life cannot exist without death and creation cannot occur without chaos and destruction.

All of the runes, all of the time, hold balance.
They are neither good nor bad.
Whenever a rune is present, it carries all of its truth. It is not necessary to worry about whether it is reversed, inverted, or upside down. All the runes hang in the cosmos just like the earth hangs suspended in space. There is no up or down, bottom or top. There is no positive or negative. Life just is.

Because Laguz belongs to water, it is a rune that is often associated with emotions. There is a tendency to judge and categorize emotions as being good or bad, positive or negative, much in the same way that we judge gentle, flowing water as good and powerful, destructive water as bad. All emotions exist for a reason. They alert us to situations that require a response. When we try to push our so-called negative emotions away, or try to eliminate them or overcome them, we may very well be pushing away the information we need to know in order to respond appropriately to a situation that could kill us.

Often the determination of good and bad is based on moralizing and the runes are not moral. They just are. So the appearance of Laguz provides a great opportunity to

pay attention to what we are feeling, without judgment, and then explore the wisdom we are being given.
What happens to you when you judge your emotions?
What benefits can you gain from viewing all emotions as equal instead of categorizing them?

Whenever I connect with Laguz there is a question that always bubbles up.
Is there a rune for salt water?
Our Northern European ancestors were surrounded by salt water. They were sea-faring explorers. They had gods and goddesses whose homes were in the ocean. They gave personal names to different kinds of ocean waves, referring to them collectively as Wave Maidens, the nine daughters of Ran and Aegir.
Does it not seem strange that there is no rune specifically for salt water?
What are your feelings?
Does Laguz encompass all water, fresh, salt, brackish, flowing?
There is a rune for ice and one for hail.
Why are there not any runes for rain, or snow, or fog or mist?
Is there an absence?
Is there a presence?

It is not possible to run out of water. It is a closed system. It does not go any place. It cannot. All that happens is constant relocation.
Water is held in underground aquifers.

Water is held in polar ice caps.
Water is suspended in the atmosphere.
All rivers flow to the ocean.
All water returns to the earth.

fully aroused by her mound
the honored doorway
the sacred
mystery of stored seed
bursts forth
blessing the mother
brother sister lover
with gifts
ancestor to kings
Ingwaz
engorged
I follow your wagon

 INGWAZ

I have a particular fondness for this rune because of its connection to my name, Ingrid, which means the beauty or loveliness of Ing. My mother Sigrid gave me the name and it connects me to my Swedish heritage, as well as to the rune Ingwaz and the god Ing. He is one of the many gods of my pre-Christian, European ancestors. Ingvi Freyr is the mystery of stored seed that bursts forth, blessing the earth. He is the lover of his twin sister, Freya, and it is their union that keeps alive the unbroken bloodlines of the ancestors.

When Ing rides into your life on his chariot pulled by wild boars, he is quite impressive. He can arouse and awaken feelings of virility and potency, fecundity and fertility, male and female sexual and creative energies.

He is the fully erect phallus aroused by the fully engorged female.

He will look around and demand to know where in your home and in your life you have made a place for him, a place of honor, a sacred space, an altar.

At the homes of so many people of European ancestry, he is met by Tibetan prayer flags, statues of Buddha, pictures of the Virgin Mary and Jesus, symbols of Om or images of Shiva and Shakti, two Hindu gods.

But rarely, if ever, does he find a home where he is represented or even recognized. We are all suffering from the absence and dishonoring of Ingwaz.

What has happened to us that we have lost connection with the gods and goddesses of our own European ancestry but know instead the mythology of our Roman conquerors? Why are we more familiar with the ideologies of Eastern religions, and the spiritual practices and traditions of Native Americans than we are with our own indigenous heritage? We are so disconnected we no longer remember that Europeans lived rich, diversified, and deeply spiritual lives, long before Christianity.

It is time to bring Ingvi Freyr back into our lives and place him in the peaceful inglenook beside our hearth.

It is time to remember the sacred gifts of the household

gods, the blessing of the home, the health and fertility of the family, the livestock and the land, and the creative fire of full arousal and sexual passion.

Where in your home and life do you honor this ancestral god?

While working with this rune I have been shown that there are times when Ingwaz can be twisted together and pulled so tight that the central, container shape is closed down. This is similar to the tangling of yarn, from separate balls, that twists together and forms knots. When the container shape is twisted shut, it prevents the energy of Ing from being used for orgasm, fertility, birth and creativity. It needs to be opened up and this can be done by following Ing's wagon as it is pulled in procession around the circuit, formed by the shape of the Gar rune, which is formed when Gebo is overlaid on Ingwaz.

I have seen this pattern superimposed on the land of the British Isles.

I follow the wagon as it is pulled around the circuit.

Do you?

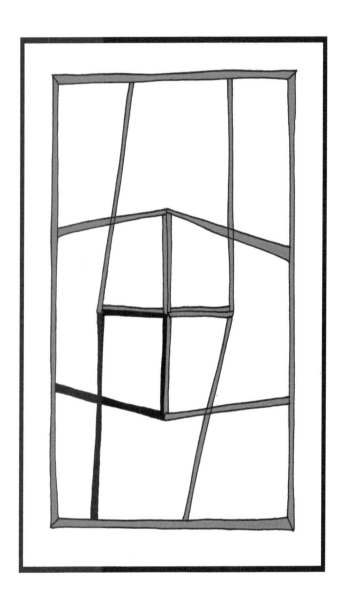

Othila
I carry you
in my body
you have fed me
the bones of my ancestors
unto you
I offer up the blood legacy
for future generations
held in the memory of Mimir

 OTHILA

Do you know who you are?

Do you know who your people are?

Do you know where your ancestors are buried?

These are the questions Othila asks.

We have lost our connection with ancestral home. We have wandered far and wide, and have sat at the sacred fires of many strange and foreign peoples.

We know their words but we no longer speak our Mother Tongue.

We have forgotten who we are and where we come from.

To me, this is like the children's story, written in 1960, by P. D. Eastman. *Are You My Mother?*

In this story a small bird hatches and falls from the nest while its mother is away finding food. It wanders around, from place to place, searching. It asks the same question of everyone it meets,

'Are you my mother?'

In the end, it must return to its home to find out who it is.

Most people are quite surprised when I say to them that Othila reminds us that we eat our ancestors. They birthed us and fed us and they still feed us through the cycle of death, decomposition and return to the soil.

Imagine living on the land, in one place, long enough to be born there, die there and be buried there. Your body, returned to the earth, would be used by the earth to produce food that would feed your offspring.

That is how we carry Othila in our bodies.

Americans of British Isle and European ancestry are threshold people. We suffer from inherited ancestral grief. We have not lived long enough in the Americas to call ourselves natives and yet most of us could not return to Europe and call home the places our indigenous ancestors lived.

Sadly, many European Americans can only think of their ancestors in the context of Christianity, forgetting the rich and diversified spiritual heritage that was destroyed by monotheism.

We may have forgotten with our minds but our bodies remember. We carry, in our bodies and our bones, the DNA, cellular memories of who we are and where we come from. Working with Othila, and listening to its sounds, will help us reactivate the memories of our bloodlines so we can reconnect with our ancestors and regain a sense of place.

Ancestry is important, not as a way to establish or prove superiority, but as a way to celebrate uniqueness and the vital role that diversity plays in the vibrancy and continuation of life here on earth.

I come across so many people whose only focus seems to be past lives and so often these lives were supposedly lived in places really foreign to that person's ancestry. I question why it is that so many who claim knowledge of past lives also claim to have been someone famous or special or belonged to a group that has been singled out in history. Does anyone ever remember a past life that was just ordinary and day-to-day?

Did everyone sit at the feet of Jesus or sail on a boat with Cleopatra or die during the burning times?

Why not spend some time following the threads of Wyrd back to where your people come from?

Perhaps Othila can lead you back to Mimir, The Rememberer, who grew into the mountain of stone, whose head was severed, and from whose mouth the Well of Wisdom pours forth. Odin gave one of his eyes so he could see differently and remember.

What would you offer up in order to remember who you are and who your people are?

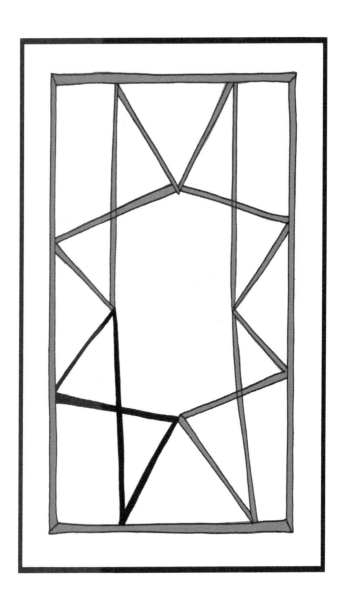

arms folded
I cross myself
the still point
constantly moving
leaving
returning
emerging
from light darkness
where they meet
am I willing
to be nothing
Dagaz the double edge
brings death and birth

DAGAZ

There are some rune books that refer to Dagaz as the rune
of daybreak. I suggest you look at its shape. It is a rune of
wholeness. To name it daybreak is to speak of only half of
it. It holds the energy of extremes, of both ends, both daybreak and nightfall. It is balanced and it is even, and there
is a place in the middle where the two extremes come
together and at that point neither of them exists. They are
both nothing.

Dagaz contains both sunset and sunrise, the power of night and day, dark and light, as well as the point of intersection, the still point, the threshold, the liminal space.

It is interesting that in the English language the word day is used to include both day and night. Have you ever thought about that?

We are all familiar with using the expression 'an entire day' to describe a 24-hour period.

Why do we not say instead, 'an entire night'?

Is it because we fear the dark?

If Dagaz holds both dark and light, we could easily call it the rune of nightfall and be just as correct as when we call it the rune of daybreak. But such singular descriptions misrepresent the energies of the rune.

I read an explanation once about the Dagaz rune where the writer said,

> "darkness isn't darkness. It's a quality of the light."

I find that statement extremely strange. And stranger still when attempting to apply it to the ancient wisdom of Dagaz. Dark is not a quality of light any more than light is a quality of dark. Darkness is not the absence of light any more than light is the absence of darkness.

Many times when Dagaz appears in a reading, it comes as an invitation to examine your own relationship with and beliefs around darkness.

Do you avoid darkness or even using the word dark?

Are you perpetually speaking about and seeking only light?

Do you consider darkness to be bad, negative, or something to avoid?

Are you out of harmony with Dagaz because of your own thinking?

Dagaz will show itself in times of transformation. Often I use the example of the metamorphosis of the caterpillar. For a certain period of time, all the caterpillar does is eat. Then at some moment it stops and begins to create, from its own body, a container that will enclose it and during the time of confinement it will go through a complete change in form. The body of the caterpillar begins to liquefy and it reaches the place where it is not a caterpillar or a butterfly. It is not one thing or the other. It is nothing and it is no thing. It has reached the still point of the Dagaz rune, the point just before the turning. Everything that was needed to become something new was contained within the old, and all that is needed to become again the old, is contained within the new.

Once transformed, the butterfly must emerge from the container and to do so requires movement and persistence. And once it emerges, it must trust that its newly formed wings will allow it to fly.

Powerful, transformative things happen in the dark. It

takes stored energy and information to transform and it
takes stored energy and information to emerge.

There are times during the process of transformation
that require stillness and waiting. There are times during
the process of transformation that require persistence
and determination.

Do you allow yourself to be still in order to transform?
Do you know how to effort in order to emerge?
What can you learn from Dagaz?

Dagaz holds the energy of birth because it is a transition
from one space into another through a narrow passage.
Dagaz holds the energy of death because it is a transition
from one space into another through a narrow passage.

Does the light emerge from the darkness or does the dark-
ness emerge from the light?
Or do both things happen?
How do you answer?

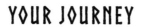

YOUR JOURNEY

Coming into relationship with the runes requires slowing down, paying attention, noticing, observing and listening. Once you decide you want to know them and form relationships with them, you will begin to see their shapes in your day-to-day life.

When you see a rune, take note and ask yourself some questions.

Where am I?

What is happening around me and around the rune right now?

What am I thinking, wondering or worrying about?

Am I going, coming or returning?

Do I need to pay attention to something?

To truly know the runes you must stop thinking of them as mere symbols or an alphabet. The rune staves are the individual signatures of spirit beings who embody timeless wisdom and who are eager to connect with you once you acknowledge their existence. It is not any different from your relationships with other humans. You cannot really get to know someone by reading about them. You can learn the basics but to really form a connection, you must get to know them through relationship.

If you ever come to a place, when working with the runes, that you feel stuck or confused, do not automatically reach for a book to find an explanation. Go instead to the rune itself and ask it what it wants you to know.

And then listen.

Another aspect of knowing the runes is becoming familiar with their shapes. I recommend that you get some graph paper and begin to draw the runes, making patterns with them. Draw them in different directions. Attach them. Overlay them. You will quickly notice how they repeat each other and how one rune can be seen in the shapes of other runes.

For instance, Laguz can be seen in Teiwaz and Ansuz. Gebo forms part of Ior as well as Gar and Ingwaz sits on top of Kenaz to form Othila. Yr is made from the strength of Uruz holding the stillness of Isa.

You can also form relationships through sound. Each rune carries its own characteristic vibration. They are distinctively individual, like musical instruments. Alone they play their own music. Placed together, they become an orchestra, making a harmonious sound.

Explore various ways to create visceral relationships with the runes by using your body to repeat their shapes and then making their sounds while holding the pose. When you feel their vibrations in your body, you will quickly know when you are in harmony and just as quickly know when you are out of tune.

All of the rune shapes can be collapsed into single, straight lines that can be stacked on top of each other and placed on the Isa Rune. Imagine this to be like the layers of snow and ice that stack on top of each other, year after year, forming glaciers. Isa is the rune of ice so it should come as no surprise that as the ice is melting at this time in history, more and more runes are being revealed and some of them may be revealing themselves to you.

Be open to the possibility that you may see shapes that are not currently considered to be runes. If you do see something, do not discount it or discard it. Draw it and make a note of what it feels like to you, and perhaps write down any thoughts or sensations that have come along with it.

As the ice is melting, the runes are being revealed.

WHISPERS

Have you ever heard anyone speak about being separated from source?

As if source is someone or something from which we can be separated.

And if it is true that we can be separated, were do we go when that happens?

It seems to me that such an expression carries with it an underlying belief in some sort of hierarchy or dominant, supreme being who is the creator and such a belief is certainly not what the runes are about. Most often when I hear someone speak about source, I detect a taint of monotheism.

It is my belief that the runes have always existed and have been witnesses to chaos and order over and over again. Each rune makes its own unique sound and each sound is necessary to the harmonious music of the whole, the music of the universe as well as the music that is played through each of us individually.

When we see a rune shape, we are, in fact, seeing a recognizable sound, not unlike seeing musical notes written on a staff.

Ginnungagap is humming a great song. As we begin to learn and recognize the shapes of the runes, we begin to know their names and when we speak their names we make their sounds and in making their sounds we can tune with them.

So I have a question and that should come as no surprise. I always have questions.

Why would there be a religion that forbids its followers to say the name of their god?

It seems to me that saying the name, which is also making the sound, is a way to stay strong, in harmony and connected.

Who benefits from such a prohibition?

Does it serve to keep the people weak and more easily enslaved, under the control of the monotheistic high god?

Who benefits from us not making the sound of the name?

Perhaps the danger that exists in the speaking of the name is that once the name is spoken the people will remember who the god really is, not who he wants them to believe he is.

There is a scripture that speaks about the spirit of god moving across the surface of the great watery deep. Using the imagery that things are spoken into existence, I am wondering if the expression 'moving across the surface of the waters' could be referring to the sounds of creation or the speaking of creation. We cannot see sound but we can see the effects of sound. Sounds can cause water to ripple.

What if these sounds, moving across the water, were sounds made by runes?

Could that explain how it was possible for Odin to see the runes in the water of the Well?

Throughout the ages, there have been times of warming and times of freezing on the earth, times when there were inland seas in the middle of the United States and times when ice reached all the way down into the British Isles.

When the water froze in times past, is it possible that the sounds of the runes were preserved in suspension, in the ice? As the ice is currently melting, are some of the long-forgotten runes being released?

When we see these revealed shapes and learn their names, are we seeing and hearing the ancient sounds of creation?

Did the melting of ice so long ago make sounds, not unlike the creaking and groaning of the great glaciers that are calving today?

Are the sounds we are hearing today, as the ice melts, sounds that existed in the past, sounds that were moving over the surface of the waters?

Are they sounds of creation and have they been held suspended in the ice waiting to be released at a time of new beginnings?

And as they are being released, will we see them as new rune shapes?

Has that been the purpose of Isa and of the ice?

Did the water in the Well, where Odin saw some of the runes, come from the melting of the ice of Niflheim when it collided with the fires of Muspelheim?

Could we say that here on earth, at this time, the spirits of the gods are moving again across the surface of the watery deep?

Was the expression 'the spirit of the lord' a way to describe the breath of creation?

Is the great song of the universe present at all times of creation and was that great song breathed into the waters that cover the earth?

If that is true then the sounds of creation are held within the endless rhythms of the freezing and thawing of the waters and they are held and released with each cycle of creation and destruction.

Rather than embracing a belief that we can be separated from source, which indicates a beginning, why not consider the possibility that we are all eternally part of the whole, that everything has always been because there is no beginning and no ending and there is no place to go. We are already here.

What actually is the Void, Ginnungagap?
What is in it?
Do the Nornir dwell there?

Do the sounds of runes exist in it?

Were the sounds of the runes woven by the Nornir onto and into the Web of the Wyrd and then placed in the water as shapes so we could see them?

Does water give us the ability to see sound?

Is that why the ice had to melt?

Did Muspelheim and Niflheim exist in the Gap or were they some place else?

What about the Wells?

Where were they?

They are said to be located in the roots of Yggdrasil, the World Tree.

So does the Tree exist in the Gap?

Has it always been there?

Did the realms of fire and ice exist before the Tree or were they in the Tree?

Were the Wells formed from the waters of the melting ice?

The Wells are said to exist in the roots.

Mimir's Well is in the realm of the frost giants.

Urd's Well is in the realm of Asgard.

Hvelgimir is in Niflheim.

If the Wells are in the roots and Urd's Well is in Asgard, does that mean that Asgard is in the roots of the World Tree?

And if so, why is it shown in the branches?

Is that because the high gods imagine themselves to be above?

Are the branches simply a mirror image of the roots?

Nothing I say is true.
Everything I say is true.
The truth lives in the questions.

THE POEMS

The 33 rune poems contained in this book were written by Ingrid Kincaid and first appeared in the (un) familiar, a limited edition, completely handmade, art book. Handmade paper, formed in a custom mold, was hand stitched into hand cut cowhide covers. Only 33 copies were letterpress printed using hand set type.

Each poem consists of only 33 words, written without punctuation. They can be read top to bottom, bottom to top, forward and backward, or even alternating the lines. The poems are alive so their meanings can change with each reading.

The book was released in March 2014.
All 33 of the original copies have been sold.

The story of the creation of the poems as well as the creation of the original book can be found on Ingrid's website: IngridKincaid.com

THE CARDS

The deck consists of 66 cards

33 rune poems

33 rune illustrations

The instructions included with the deck are:

the right way is (un) familiar

the wrong way is (un) familiar

the way you choose is (un) familiar

the way you are chosen is (un) familiar

you will know the way

you will be shown the way

only as you use it

The deck can be purchased with the book or separately.
Use them how you wish.

The runes are not about fortune telling or predicting the future.

They carry and impart wisdom. They vibrate with the knowing of what has been, what is present, and what, by necessity, will unfold.

You participate in all of this.

Change one thing and everything changes.

If you plant an acorn, you can expect an oak tree to grow.

Oak trees grow from acorns.

Acorns grow into oak trees.

Apple seeds grow into apple trees.

Apple trees grow apples with seeds.

Kernels of rye will not produce a crop of barley.

If you do not want an oak tree, do not plant an acorn.

If you planted an acorn, do not complain or be surprised when the oak starts to grow.

If you want something else, plant it.

However, all that being said, there might be times when you plant an acorn and nothing grows.

The acorn might be defective.

It might get dug up and eaten by squirrels.

It might get washed away in a flood.

The soil might not be conducive to growth.

There are some things in life over which we have no control and there are some things in life we participate in and affect by the choices we make.

Listen to the runes as they vibrate with what is, which determines what will be and eventually becomes that which has been. You get to decide whether or not you want to play the music of your life in harmony or out of tune.

May the cards and the book support you on your (un) familiar journey.

Nothing is as it seems.

ᚠ ᚦ ᛗ ᛏ ᚲ ᛁ ᚺ ᚷ ᚹ

BIOS

ABOUT THE AUTHOR

I am the daughter of Arctic glaciers, rocky shorelines and windswept moors. I was born knowing the runes. They're etched in my bones. They're my lineage, my ancestry, my bloodlines. Their wisdom informs all that I do. People in the community know me as the rune woman.

I'm wise and irreverent, pragmatic and intuitive.

The power of my work as an author, teacher and spiritual guide is found in the questions I'm willing to ask, questions that are challenging, controversial and rarely politically correct. I invite you to consider what would happen in your life if you asked different questions.

This book, THE RUNES REVEALED, is a companion text to an online course of the same name. Visit my website to discover all that I have to offer: classes, rituals, online courses and private, spiritual guidance. IngridKincaid.com

ABOUT THE ILLUSTRATOR

I am a maker, an artist and writer rooted in nature, spirit, ritual and empowerment.

My vision is at the intersection of spirit and place. I seek to collaborate and co-create work that is handmade, divinely guided, honoring to earth rhythms and the ancestors. Working with the runes has helped me re-member my lineage relationships and connect with the land where I currently reside. My offerings include custom place portraits, rune mandalas, divination tools and illuminated books. For commissions or to connect with me visit laravesta.co.

CPSIA information can be obtained
at www.ICGtesting.com
Printed in the USA
FSHW01n0249300718
50825FS